LATIN AMERICAN HISTORY GOES TO THE MOVIES

Latin American History Goes to the Movies combines the study of the rich history of Latin America with the medium of feature film. In this concise and accessible book, author Stewart Brewer helps readers understand key themes and issues in Latin American history, from pre-Columbian times to the present, by examining how they have been treated in a variety of films. Moving chronologically across Latin American history, and pairing historical background with explorations of selected films, the chapters cover vital topics including the Spanish conquest and colonialism, revolution, religion, women, US–Latin American relations, and more. Through films such as *City of God*, *Frida*, and *Che*, Brewer shows how history is retold, and what that retelling means for public memory.

From *Apocalypto* to *Selena*, and from Christopher Columbus to the slave trade, *Latin American History Goes to the Movies* sets the record straight between the realities of history and cinematic depictions, and gives readers a solid foundation for using film to understand the complexities of Latin America's rich and vibrant history.

Stewart Brewer is Professor of History at Metropolitan Community College in Omaha, Nebraska.

LATIN AMERICAN HISTORY GOES TO THE MOVIES

Understanding Latin America's Past through Film

Stewart Brewer

Routledge
Taylor & Francis Group

NEW YORK AND LONDON

First published 2016
by Routledge
711 Third Avenue, New York, NY 10017

And by Routledge
2 Park Square, Milton Park, Abingdon, Oxon OX14 4RN

Routledge is an imprint of the Taylor & Francis Group, an informa business

© 2016 Taylor & Francis

Library of Congress Cataloging-in-Publication Data
Brewer, Stewart, 1971–
    Latin American history goes to the movies : understanding Latin America's past through film / Stewart Brewer.
        pages cm
    Includes index.
    1. Latin America—In motion pictures.   2. History in motion pictures.
3. Latin Americans in motion pictures.   I. Title.
    PN1995.9.L37B74 2015
    791.43′628–dc23
    2015016545

ISBN: 978-0-415-87350-5 (hbk)
ISBN: 978-0-415-87351-2 (pbk)
ISBN: 978-1-315-68588-5 (ebk)

Typeset in Bembo
by Apex CoVantage, LLC

For Shannon and Brooke, Kim and Sue

CONTENTS

ACKNOWLEDGMENTS

The idea for this book began many years ago when I taught briefly at Rhodes College in Memphis, Tennessee. One of the professors there, Dr. Michael LaRosa, frequently taught a course called Latin American History through Film. I was very intrigued by this idea, and over the next several years, I developed my own course based on this concept. While teaching at Dana College in Blair, Nebraska, I offered a course on this topic for many years. The class was well-received and students generally enjoyed it, even if they occasionally grumbled about their daily writing assignments that corresponded with the films.

However, one of my largest frustrations while teaching this course was the absence of a text on Latin American history and filmography that I could have my students use in class. I was left to cobble together readings from various sources, or assign textbooks that were only marginally related to the daily topics. My search took me to numerous books on Latin American cinema, but finding a book that blended Latin American history with films about that history was difficult. I read Donald F. Stevens' book *Based on a True Story: Latin American History at the Movies* (Rowman & Littlefield, 1998), which approached what I was looking for, but I still wanted something that blended more history with more viewing options. I decided that the field needed a book that focused specifically on Latin American history as portrayed on film: a text that delivered the background historical knowledge needed to understand the topics in the films, and a text that also provided instructors with options for classroom viewing instead of tying professors to just one film per topic. I pondered this idea in my mind for a while, but my involvement in other projects and classes meant that my thoughts stayed on the backburner.

Then, one January while attending the annual conference of the American Historical Association, a colleague of mine, Dr. Iain Anderson, casually mentioned to me that he had met someone who might be interested in my book idea; this was Kimberly Guinta, then senior editor in history at Routledge. As she and I communicated about the idea over the next several months, it solidified into a formal proposal and then eventually a contracted book. Work continued, and what began as a general, imprecise idea evolved into this book that I am now very gratified to contribute to the field of literature on this topic.

This project would not have happened without the reassurance and enthusiasm of a few key individuals. I am grateful to Genevieve Aoki, senior editorial assistant at Routledge, and Margo Irvin, Commissioning Editor on US History, also at Routledge, who have been very supportive in the final stages of this project and seeing it through to completion. I am also exceptionally appreciative of Sue Williamson, who cheered, coaxed, and commended me as this project proceeded. She read each chapter as I wrote them, and reinvigorated me throughout the writing and editing process. But ultimately, this book would have never come to completion without the kind and thoughtful efforts of Kim Guinta. Her support, enthusiasm, and fervor for this book were the most important reasons for its completion. I am indebted to her for her tenacity and persistence in reassuring me to drive this project forward to conclusion.

Finally, I would be very remiss if I didn't mention the support of family and friends. Shannon and Brooke Brewer were always understanding and positive throughout the writing process. I would also like to thank Steve and Sue Howe, and Ken and Joan Kratt for their reassurances and encouragement along the way. Tom Pearcy made helpful comments at the inception of the project, and Garrett Oleen lent a hand with recommendations of Spanish-language films. Many other people also had a hand in this project at one stage or another along the line, and to name them all would be impossible. But I agree with the quote attributed to Isaac Newton, "If I have seen further, it is by standing on the shoulders of giants." I thank you all, knowing that gratitude is not enough.

1

STEREOTYPES OF LATIN AMERICA

It seems unlikely that there could be any other region of the earth in which nature and human behavior could have combined to produce a more unhappy and hopeless background for the conduct of human life than in Latin America.

George F. Kennan, United States ambassador

Introduction

What is a stereotype? Stereotypes are attempts to normalize or oversimplify a society or culture based on the actions of only some of the members of that society. Stereotyping takes place both from inside and outside of a society or culture. For these reasons, cultures and groups that find themselves the object of stereotyping often deem the results to be offensive because stereotyping tends to focus on the ridiculous, negative, sensational, and outrageous elements of the culture in question. The quote that begins this chapter is a disturbing example of how stereotyping a culture or region can have negative repercussions. In this instance, United States ambassador George F. Kennan made this derogatory comment in 1950 after visiting several Latin American countries. His report (*Foreign Relations of the United States*, 1950, Volume II, pp. 598–624) contains harsh statements, accusations, and comparisons between Latin America and the United States, where he finds Latin America wanting in every way. His visit seems to have had a negative effect on his perceptions of Latin America as a whole, even though he acknowledged that his views were "shots in the dark, based mainly on instinct and general experience." But these kinds of judgments are exactly what people who desire to learn about the history of Latin America need to avoid.

For example, for people in Latin America, Europe, Asia, or other places in the world, individuals in the United States might be viewed as loud, fat, prudish, fried-food-eating, gun-packing cowboys. Few Americans would find this assessment accurate or pleasant. But there it is. How do you argue with a stereotype? George F. Kennan's attitudes about the peoples of Latin America were not new in 1950, and these opinions have existed since the beginnings of relations between the peoples of North and South America.

Stereotyping usually involves both ethnocentrism (the idea that one's own culture and way of life is superior to that of another), and the practice of intolerance (treating people in other societies as inferior). Author Charles Ramírez Berg has argued that the way to fight against prejudice is through knowledge, both about what stereotyping is, and also knowledge about the culture being judged. He states: "The first beneficial result of learning about the process of stereotyping is that this knowledge makes it easy to detect stereotypes" (Ramírez Berg 2002: 23).

Stereotypes are likely to categorize individuals into neat little boxes. Stereotypes about most cultures, including Latin Americans, tend to focus on several key associations such as race, behavior, morality, and other areas. Racially, Latin Americans are frequently portrayed as dark-skinned and dark-haired. They are depicted behaviorally as violent, passionate, and devious. Finally, Latin Americans are occasionally illustrated to have low, or no, morals, and to even undermine the moral fabric of society in general. Ramírez Berg goes on to identify several stereotypes that define Latin American characters in American films. These include characters such as bandits, prostitutes, buffoons, and male and female seducers (Ramírez Berg 2002: 66). In many of the films discussed in this book, these characteristic stereotypes are evident and often blatant.

Perceptions of Latin America

In 1992, historian Fredrick Pike wrote a book on Latin American stereotypes under the broad umbrella of US–Latin American relations. He argued, that based on the perceptions of the early inhabitants of North America, Latin Americans appeared to be more comfortable living in nature instead of manipulating and controlling nature as Americans and Europeans did. Continuing on, Pike continued by positing that Latin Americans were often judged to be more feminine and less masculine because of this relationship with the natural world around them. Some might wonder about Pike's inclusion of gender in his argument; what could gender have to do with nature? Pike argued that stereotyping along gender lines was an apt comparison from which to define the realities of US–Latin American relations: the US took the role of the male—controlling, dominant, and overriding—while Latin America took the part of the female—submissive, accepting, compliant, and yielding. The problem with this analogy is that it is based on the stereotypical assumptions of US culture as well as its relationship with Latin American nations through time.

Anthropologists and sociologists, along with historians, all use the concept of The Other to understand the phenomenon that occurs when two cultures bump up against each other. Misunderstandings are bound to happen, and this is where stereotypes are born. Looking at history, society, culture, and lifestyle from the perspective of some other group or individual is difficult but necessary if we are to truly understand what we experience, and if we desire to avoid making stereotypical mistakes in judging other people and cultures.

How and where did stereotypes of Latin American culture emerge? The early years of the nineteenth century saw the first long-term interactions between the Spanish colonies in Latin America and the United States. They had experienced brief exchanges prior to the turn of the century, but after 1800 these relations increased. In 1803, the US purchased the Louisiana Territory from France, which gave the US and Latin America their first long-distance border in North America. This border ran from the Mississippi River in the Gulf of Mexico, all the way to the Canadian border, encompassing the future US states between the Mississippi River and the Rocky Mountains. In 1823, US president James Monroe issued his famous Monroe Doctrine speech that would shape US policy in the Western Hemisphere for the next 150 years. This speech (which was actually his annual State of the Union Address) became the keystone of American political attitudes toward Latin America and it attempted to relegate Latin America to the position of a subordinate to the dominance of the United States. In the speech, President Monroe states:

> We owe it, therefore, to candor and to the amicable relations existing between the United States and [Europe] to declare that we should consider any attempt on their part to extend their system [of government] to any portion of this hemisphere as dangerous to our peace and safety. With the existing colonies or dependencies of any European power we have not interfered and shall not interfere, but with the Governments [sic] who have declared their independence and maintained it, and whose independence we have, on great consideration and on just principles, acknowledged, we could not view any interposition for the purpose of oppressing them, or controlling in any other manner their destiny, by any European power in any other light than as the manifestation of an unfriendly disposition toward the United States.
>
> *(President James Monroe, Washington, DC, December 2, 1823)*

The "Governments" he refers to are the newly created independent nations of Latin America that won their independence from Spain over more than a decade, beginning with Mexico, whose independence movement began in 1810, to Bolivia and Peru, who won their freedom by 1825. In effect, President Monroe stated that the future of the Western Hemisphere would be determined by the United States and its interactions with the new countries of Latin America.

Early contacts with the newly formed Latin American nations were brief and mostly political in nature. It was not until the 1840s and the Mexican War that individual, one-on-one relationships between Americans and Latin Americans began to take place much more frequently in places such as Texas and California. From these locations and others inside Mexico, the seeds of Latin American stereotyping were born. And as with all stereotypes, one must ask, how representative were Texas and California for the whole of Latin America in the hemisphere? The answer makes it clear that perceptions about Latin Americans as a whole were based on a small percentage of the population, in one corner of the Latin American territory. Furthermore, the populations of Texas and California, while similar in some ways to the culture and society of Mexico, Colombia, Argentina, and other countries, were themselves a separate microcosm of those cultures because of their sparse population, their distance from settled urban centers such as Mexico City, and the harsh terrain and climate that they lived in. In other words, how closely did the populations of Texas and California represent Latin America? The answer is obvious and from interactions between Americans and Latin Americans in these locations, negative stereotypes were born.

It seems that even though the years of the nineteenth century brought Americans and Latin Americans into closer contact with each other, this contact did not engender a greater sensitivity to Latin American culture on the part of the United States. In fact, the opposite seems to have occurred, where the US became more and more critical of life south of its border, and the Latin American population bore the brunt of American disregard.

Stereotyping is destructive to cultural sensitivity. When one subscribes to a stereotype about another culture, group, or society, they never get below the surface to see what lies beneath. Stereotypes damage cultural relations between groups because they prevent individuals and societies from viewing other groups in their rich, native colors, and instead pass off other cultures in terms of their inferiority to the original group, thus preventing any further understanding from taking place.

Filmography

Among the multitudes of films that could have been included in this chapter, three seem to embody the qualities and stereotypes that are found in numerous films about Latin American history and society. *Once Upon a Time in Mexico*, *¡Three Amigos!*, and *Bananas* are all outlandish and excessive in their portrayals of Latin American culture in general, Latin Americans in particular, and they play upon the preconceived notions that American audiences have already acquired about Latin America through the media. Nevertheless, they all contain multiple stereotypical characters and settings that are easy to see and are accessible to criticism and analysis. The purpose of including these films here isn't so much to show real history, but to illustrate the practice of stereotyping in an obvious manner; the plot becomes somewhat irrelevant and the films become a vehicle for studying how Latin America is frequently portrayed on the screen.

Once Upon a Time in Mexico *(2003)*

Once Upon a Time In Mexico (2003) is the story of an individual named Mariachi, which in itself is a stereotype, since his name is also the name of a widespread Latin dance and style of music. This individual, Mariachi, is a very accomplished guitar player and gunslinger. The purpose of the film is pure entertainment set against a Mexican backdrop. It is full of stereotypes from start to finish, from the quintessential Mexican gunman and his friends, to the American CIA agent, to the ambitious calculating female character, to the over-the-top action and violence. And while there is no historical significance to the film at all, it does serve in an academic sense to prepare students of Latin American history through film to observe, notice, and deconstruct stereotypes in film. It should be noted that *Once Upon a Time in Mexico* is the third film in the *Mexico Trilogy* (preceded by *El Mariachi* (1992) and *Desperado* (1995)), directed and produced by Robert Rodriguez.

At the beginning of the film, Mariachi lives in a small village that supports itself making and selling guitars. Eventually, the stereotypical "bad guys" come to get Mariachi and he decides to go with them if they agree not to harm the people of the village. Mariachi, played by Antonio Banderas, is approached by Sheldon Sands (Johnny Depp), a CIA agent, to carry out a plot to kill a high-ranking military officer, General Marquez, who in turn is attempting to assassinate the president of Mexico in a military coup. Once Mariachi agrees to help kill General Marquez, many thugs and bandits attempt to kill him on several occasions. He enters a church to meet with Sands, who is also involved in the plot against Marquez. But thugs try to kill Mariachi inside the church. With machine guns they shoot up the church and never manage to hit Mariachi, instead destroying much of the interior of the building; they destroy pews and riddle the walls with bullet holes. Mariachi scales the walls of the church interior and then reveals that his guitar has a secret compartment, where he conceals his own gun. He takes his gun out of the guitar and starts killing everyone in sight. And whereas the bad guys could never hit him, he manages to kill several of them with his superior aim. In one of the more ridiculous moments in the film, an old woman continues to pray in the church while bullets fly and mayhem continues all around her. When she finishes with her prayers, she rises to leave the church. All of the fighters cease their shooting and wait for her to leave, and then continue to kill each other when she is gone. The stereotype here is obviously playing on the notion that Mexicans are all extremely religious and extremely fierce. In one scene, the filmmakers manage to pull both of these stereotypes into one long melee of piousness and violence.

Meanwhile, the CIA agent Mariachi was supposed to meet in the church, hires another former CIA agent to help him. Depp's role in the film is murky at best. He seems to have been cast in the film to typify the American stereotype– the gringo who is oblivious to his surroundings, but has his own agenda, and is also dangerous in seeking his own ends.

Mariachi eventually seeks out some old friends who will help him with the job he has been hired to do. His two friends are also stereotypical: the young, enthusiastic but ignorant Mexican, and the older, habitually drunk Mexican. Mariachi fills his guitar case with all kinds of weapons, and then they set out to take their positions in the presidential palace where the attempted coup will take place. They play their instruments during a state dinner, posing as sideline musicians. Then, in another shootout, Mariachi kills all the present bad guys in the town square. This is followed by the obligatory chase scene, where the characters race motorcycles through a cactus field.

While these events have been taking place, Depp's character is captured by a female agent named Ajedrez (played by Eva Mendes), who was his acquaintance in the past. On the *Dia de los Muertos* (Day of the Dead), Mendes has Depp's eyes put out so that he can no longer fight. However, he uses a stereotypical street urchin boy, who sells *chicle* (gum) for a living, to help him shoot the people who are trying to kill him.

Meanwhile, Mariachi prepares for the final battle. He and his friends use remote control weapons, disguised as musical instruments, to kill people who are trying to take the president of Mexico hostage. As the climax concludes, Mariachi manages to kill General Marquez, foiling his attempted takeover of Mexico, and Depp kills Mendes's character with the help of the *chicle* boy.

The film ends in blatant stereotypical fashion; Mariachi and his friends walk down the road in slow motion, with the president of Mexico, and their instrument cases filled with money. Mariachi wears a banner displaying the flag of Mexico across his chest, and as he walks it flutters in the wind. The film concludes as Mariachi returns to his village and plays the guitar.

¡Three Amigos! *(1986)*

¡Three Amigos! (1986) is, put simply, quite silly. Again, there is absolutely no historical significance to the film, but its value for this chapter is, again, to observe stereotypes and how they are used in film to portray typical Americans and Mexicans on screen. The film takes place in Mexico in 1916. A Mexican lady rides a burro past men wearing sombreros and women in dresses. The woman enters the *Cantina del Borracho* (the Bar of the Drunk) in search of a hero. She is there searching for someone to help her and her village fight of the depredations of a Mexican bandit named *El Guapo* (The Handsome Man). The Mexican men in the bar are all very dirty and mean. They don't want to help and instead make fun of her and make sexual advances toward her.

She leaves and enters a church where she views a silent film proclaiming the deft and daring escapades of three men dressed like fancy Mexican rancheros. In the film, they deal with the bad guys and save villages. So she sends them a telegram telling them to come to Mexico and help her village deal with El Guapo. These men, who are really just actors, eventually make their way to her village, where they are welcomed with a traditional feast of rice, beans, and tortillas. Meanwhile, a German in a flight jacket shows up in the same town and shoots up the Cantina del Boracho where the woman originally went for help. He is dressed like a traditional German flying ace and he is a very accomplished sharp shooter.

El Guapo's men are dirty and they wear traditional Mexican bandit attire. They are introduced sitting on horses drinking tequila. When their alcohol runs out, they decide to go to the nearby village to get more. They bully the town into giving them tequila. By this time, the Three Amigos have arrived, but they don't realize they have been invited to fight real bandits—they think they are there to put on a show like they do in the movies. They chase the Mexican bandits off after commenting that the bandits "looked a little too cliché." Thinking that their job is over, they relax while El Guapo's men tell him about the Amigos.

Soon El Guapo returns with 50 men. The Amigos go out and put on the same show, but one of the bandits shoots Steve Martin's character in the arm, and they realize that the bandits are real and that this is not a show. At this point they run away and the bandits shoot up the town. But the Amigos soon decide to return and fight. The stereotypes come fast and furious at this point. El Guapo has a birthday party that is full of piñatas, and his compound is full of Mexican prostitutes.

After much silly fighting and interaction between Guapo's men and the Amigos, the Amigos defeat the bandits—with the help of the villagers, and then

FIGURE 1.1 *¡Three Amigos!* (1986, Orion Pictures).

ride away, having declined to take the money that the villagers offered to pay them for their great service.

The value of this film, aside from the light-hearted entertainment that borders on the ridiculous, is in the very blatant stereotypical roles of the Americans, Mexican bandits, Mexican citizens, and the German flying ace. One of the things that makes these stereotypes work so well is the fact that they have been perpetuated so frequently in other films and media. They are instantly recognizable and they help the viewer tell who is good and who is bad simply by looking at them. The danger is that each depiction further cements these stereotypes for the future. It does nothing to dispel the stereotypical roles, and in fact seems to celebrate the stereotypes for their own sake.

Bananas *(1971)*

Woody Allen's 1971 film *Bananas* is possibly one of his best early films. Here, the stereotypes in the film play on the apprehensions and fears of Americans in the 1960s and 1970s regarding Fidel Castro's regime in Cuba, and the perceived worldwide proliferation of communism. Nevertheless the stereotypes and archetypes in this film are easily recognizable more than 40 years later, although some of the jokes are now quite dated.

The film opens with one of the most brilliant skits in the whole film. Don Dunphy and Howard Cosell, two famous sportscasters of the 1960s and 1970s, are narrating a live assassination in a small, fictional Latin American dictatorship named San Marcos. This scene makes fun of Latin American politics while at the same time spoofing American reactions to Latin American affairs, reducing the assassination to the level of a spectator sport for American audiences. The president of San Marcos is gunned down on camera, and Howard Cosell coolly states that he needs to get through the crowd, and that they need to let American television get closer to the action. Cosell attempts to interview the dying president of San Marcos—much like he interviewed defeated boxers after fights in the ring, especially fighters beaten by boxer Muhammad Ali who Cosell covered for some of his most famous fights. The new dictator of San Marcos is a right-wing military general, and the opposing rebels are hiding in the hills mounting a resistance movement. All of this is reminiscent of Cuba in 1959, when Castro's resistance drove Cuban dictator Fulgencio Batista from power after mounting a long and often violent resistance campaign in the Cuban mountains.

The next 30 minutes of the film are inconsequential, dealing with Fielding Mellish's (played by Woody Allen) attempts to impress and seduce a woman. It is filled with the funny clichés and antics that Allen liked to put in some of his early films. Eventually, Mellish flies to San Marcos. There the portrayal of the ridiculous elements in Latin American continue, as the new president/dictator of San Marcos is presented with his weight in horse manure because that is the only resource the country has in abundance. After Mellish arrives in the country, he goes to a hotel that has the obligatory pictures of Jesus and the president on the wall.

Later, Mellish attends a dinner with the president, who expresses his fear of the communist rebels in the mountains. During the meal, the president and his lackeys plan to dress men as rebels and have them assassinate Mellish so that the United States will intervene militarily in the country, overthrowing the real rebels, and restoring order to the right-wing military dictatorship. In this plot twist, Allen parodies the fact that the United States has intervened militarily in Latin American countries for more than a century. Many of these interventions were planned and carried out to fight against the perceived worldwide proliferation of communism.

The assassination of Mellish is botched and he ends up joining the rebels in the mountains. They all are costumed like Fidel Castro's soldiers during the Cuban Revolution. The leader of the rebels, Esposito, looks like Castro, complete with green fatigues and a beard. Eventually, the president/dictator of San Marcos escapes to Miami (again channeling Fulgencio Batista, the Cuban leader who was ousted by Fidel Castro) and the rebels take control of the government of San Marcos. Esposito, who is now in charge of the country, declares that he will turn the government into a dictatorship because the people are not smart enough to understand political issues and vote responsibly. He decides to export bananas to the United States, mirroring the large banana companies (such as the United Fruit Company or UFCO) that exploited Central American nations during the nineteenth and twentieth centuries.

Eventually Mellish returns to the United States disguised as Esposito, but with a red beard to match his red hair. The US government decides he is trying to establish a missile base in San Marcos—reminiscent of the events of the Cuban Missile Crisis of the early 1960s. Mellish is put on trial and then pardoned, and the film ends with more silly episodes with the woman he attempted to seduce at the beginning of the film, along with a reprisal of Howard Cosell sports-casting the events in the closing scenes.

The film *Bananas* definitely has merit as a treatise on how Americans have viewed Latin America in the past. Woody Allen makes fun of these American perceptions while perpetuating some of his own as well. The point of the film seems to be that citizens of the United States do not think about Latin America very often, and when they do they have preconceived notions of what Latin America is like, and how Latin Americans act. At the same time, the films pokes fun at American culture in the United States and how Americans are materialistic and unaware of events transpiring south of their borders.

Conclusions

After viewing these three outsized examples of outlandish Latin American stereotyping, viewers should have developed solid notions of the common stereotypes employed by filmmakers to signal particular features and attitudes about Latin American culture and society. These cinematic examples should be kept in mind throughout the rest of the book, so that stereotypes, intentional and otherwise, can be identified and interpreted. Stereotypes do perpetuate commonly held assumptions about societies, and they can and often do color the way people view unfamiliar groups. But when viewed for what they are, as attempts to standardize and simplify a certain culture, viewers can move beyond the portrayal of preposterous, undesirable, and even scandalous elements of a culture, and uncover a more accurate portrait of the people and institutions in an unexperienced society and why they are perceived the way they often are.

Further Reading

Foster, Kevin. *Lost Worlds: Latin America and the Imagining of Empire.* London: Palgrave, 2009.

Pike, Fredrick. *The United States and Latin America: Myths and Stereotypes of Civilization and Nature.* Austin, TX: University of Texas Press, 1992.

Ramírez Berg, Charles. *Latino Images in Film: Stereotypes, Subversion, Resistance.* Austin, TX: University of Texas Press, 2002.

2

PRE-COLUMBIAN CULTURES

Then the sky would fall, it would fall down upon the earth, when the four gods, the four Bacabs, were set up, who brought about the destruction of the world. Then, after the destruction of the world was completed, they placed a tree to set up in its order the yellow cock oriole. Then the white tree of abundance was set up. A pillar of the sky was set up, a sign of the destruction of the world; that was the white tree of abundance in the north. Then the black tree of abundance was set up in the west for the black-breasted picoy to sit upon. Then the yellow tree of abundance was set up in the south as a symbol of the destruction of the world, for the yellow-breasted picoy to sit upon, for the yellow cock oriole to sit upon. Then the green tree of abundance was set up in the center of the world as a record of the destruction of the world.

Prophesies of Chilam Balam, Book X

Introduction

In 1492, Christopher Columbus encountered a vast, rich environment that was home to a multitude of different Native American Indian groups who spoke different languages and lived in many different geographical zones and conditions. For more than 10000 years the peoples of the Western Hemisphere had existed in virtual isolation from the Eurasian land mass, and when Europeans arrived at the end of the fifteenth century, they found civilizations in different stages of development that ranged from Stone Age hunters and gatherers, to rudimentary farmers, to Bronze Age empires that rivaled Egypt and Mesopotamia.

The Siberian ancestors of the native Latin American peoples migrated into the Western Hemisphere over a period of hundreds of years as they followed game and food sources across the Bering Strait ice bridge at the end of the Pleistocene period. When the great glaciation ended around 9000 BC, the water levels rose, making land-based migration across the Bering Strait impossible. But the Asiatic wandering tribes that had roamed into the Western Hemisphere spread throughout North and South America, and by 7000–6000 BC began to develop rudimentary agriculture in some locations. Agricultural products such as maize, means, squash, and potatoes became staples in Native American diets in Central and South America, while gathering and hunting were predominant in areas of North America, particularly along the Atlantic and Pacific coasts. In Latin America, the variety and diversity of Indian cultures and technologies astonished the Spanish explorers when they arrived at the end of the fifteenth century.

While the hemisphere was literally full of various Indian groups and cultures, the Spanish were drawn to three predominant groups because of their political sophistication, their population numbers, and—perhaps most important of all—because of their wealth. These three groups were the Maya of southern Mexico and Guatemala, the Aztecs of central Mexico, and the Inca of Peru/Bolivia who had spread throughout much of the Andean coastline of South America.

The Maya

The ancient Maya were arguable the most advanced group in the Western Hemisphere at the time of European contact in various ways. Other Indian groups such as the Aztecs and the Inca were perhaps more advanced in political sophistication, agricultural production, medicinal techniques, and warfare, but the Maya displayed rare erudition in architecture, sculpture, painting, mathematics, astronomy, calendrics, and writing. From 250 to 900AD, the Maya inhabited the Mesoamerican jungles that today comprise the modern countries of Guatemala, Belize, El Salvador, western Honduras, and Mexico's Yucatan Peninsula.

One of the primary means of food production for the Maya was slash-and-burn farming. Sometimes called *milpa* farming, slash-and-burn involved the burning of tracts of land—including the trees and all the vegetation—and then planting corn in the ash-rich soil. In this way the soil received needed nutrients that corn leached from the soil. After a few plantings, the area was permitted to remain fallow while a new tract was burned and planted in the same way. Scholars working at the Guatemalan site of Tikal have discovered evidence of farming in an area of roughly 50 square miles around the Tikal ceremonial site. Other Maya ceremonial sites such as Yaxchilàn, Palenque, Copan, and others had similar agricultural regions surrounding their pyramidal centers.

Maya political structure was less centralized than either the Aztecs or the Inca. At the top of the social order in each of the larger Maya sites was the hereditary ruler who was the embodiment of a political, military, and religious leader all in one. Under this king/priest ruler were the nobility who filled roles in administration, bureaucracy, and some specific craft specializations such as architects, priests, and scribes. These occupations were very specialized and required advanced training. As such, those who achieved such skills were considered valued members of the royal household.

Maya artisans occupied the social tier under the nobility. They used their talents and energies creating pottery, paintings, stonework, sculpture, and other acts of beautification of Maya ceremonial sites. Stone stelae decorated the edges of buildings and the grounds around palace complexes, and ornate carvings and texts covered the surfaces of many structures, requiring the work of both artisans and also the scribes mentioned above. Finally, peasant farmers comprised the bulk of the Maya population. They produced the food and manual labor upon which the Maya civilization existed. In addition to producing food from agriculture and hunting, they also provided manual labor for cutting and carrying stone for the production of the huge palace complexes and temple-pyramids that dot the Maya landscape to this day.

Maya political development was unique when compared to the Aztec and Inca Empires. The Maya were not politically centralized to the same degree and, unlike the Aztecs and Inca, the Maya did not have a single capital city. Instead, much like ancient Greece, the Maya were divided up into territories or city-states with several different city-center complexes that each housed a local royal family. These city-states traded with each other, entered into marriage alliances, and fought wars with each other on a regular basis. During the period of the Spanish conquest of Latin America, this situation proved somewhat frustrating for the Spanish because they could not duplicate their feats of conquest in the Maya area as they had done in the Aztec and Inca regions. For the centralized Aztec and Inca Empires, the Spanish went for the top-level leadership and imposed their order on the political structure from the top down. In the Maya area, the Spanish had to fight over and over against each city-state because there was no top-level capital or king to topple that would bring the whole apparatus down as it had in the Aztec and Inca Empires.

Warriors could come from any of the social levels, but were predominantly from the upper levels of the royal families and the nobility. War was considered an occupation much like the farming, carving, or painting done by Maya artisans. Specific times of year were designated as times of war by the precise Maya calendar, and these were the times of year when the warriors would engage fighters from other city-states in combat. The goal of Maya warfare was not to kill as many of the enemy as possible, but rather to capture the enemy soldiers in hand-to-hand combat. These war captives were then used as slaves, bargaining chips, sacrificial victims, and as rewards to be bestowed by Maya rulers on worthy warriors, nobles, and others.

Maya religion was polytheistic and a multitude of gods were worshipped on a daily basis. With names such as Itzam-Na, Tlaloc, Kukulcan, Xipe, and others, Maya deities presided over specific natural phenomena and seasons. Various elaborate ceremonies were performed, sometimes daily, to placate the gods and appease them so that they would aid the Maya in their needs and desires. Gods of the sky and the underworld could be helpful, but also capricious at times, and fickle in their desire to aid the Maya. Therefore, ceremonial actions and offerings were essential in gaining the approbation of the gods.

Maya religious ceremonies consisted of various practices that ranged from simple fasting and consumption of hallucinogenic drugs, to bloodletting and human sacrifice. For the Maya, blood was sacred, and the practice of human sacrifice on a massive scale—as took place among the Aztecs—was not as prevalent. Instead, bloodletting seems to have been more widespread as a religious appeasement for the Maya deities. Bloodletting was practiced by royals in sacred spaces atop temples and pyramids. The individual or individuals who were to perform the ritual would pierce various locations on their bodies (common locations for Maya bloodletting were earlobes, tongues, and penises) with stingray spines and other sharp objects. The blood from these puncture wounds was collected on bark paper and burned along with incense as an offering to the gods.

All of these religious ritual offerings and sacrifices were dictated by the magnificent Maya calendar, a 52-year cycle of permuting calendar systems that directed the civic and religious life of Maya civilization. One of the calendars that comprised the Maya calendrical system was the sacred calendar, which was made up of the combination of 20 day names with 13 numbers, giving this calendar a cycle of 260 days. The other calendar was the regular yearly calendar that repeated every 365 days. When these two calendars were combined, they formed the Calendar Round, a system that did not repeat until a period of 52 years had passed away. The Maya calendar was essential for predicting times for planting, harvesting, warfare, reproduction, and sacrifice.

Around 800AD, classical Maya civilization went through a mysterious collapse that entailed the cessation of massive construction, carving of monuments and stelae, and the abandonment of the massive jungle ceremonial centers. For many years, scholars were at a loss to explain this collapse, but recent scholarship indicates that population pressure, food shortage, warfare, and disaffection by the lower classes all seem to have played a role in the devolution of Maya civilization. But, while this collapse of sorts took place in the highlands of Guatemala, to the north in Mexico's Yucatan Peninsula, Maya culture and civilization continued to thrive as before with a few changes wrought by contact with the valley of central Mexico. When the Spanish arrived in Yucatan in the early 1500s, they found the Maya living and practicing their religion and agriculture much the way they had for hundreds of years.

The Aztecs

Unlike the Maya civilization that had existed for more than 1500 years, the Aztecs functioned as an empire for around 100 years before they were conquered by the Spanish. The Aztecs arrived in central Mexico around 1281, coming from northern Mexico. They claimed to be led by their principal deity, the bloody and militaristic god Huitzilopochtli. After several bloody and cruel skirmishes with surrounding Indian groups, the Aztecs settled on an island in the middle of Lake Texcoco in 1344, and began to construct their fabulous, wealthy capital city, Tenochtitlán.

The Aztec Empire—the period when the Aztecs dominated militarily and economically all of the other Indian groups in central Mexico—began in 1428. The Aztecs demanded tribute payments frequently, and swiftly doled out punishments for recalcitrant towns and villages. By the time the Spanish arrived in central Mexico in the early 1500s, it is estimated that the population of the mighty empire numbered roughly 25 million.

How the Aztecs fed their people has been a matter of serious scholarship and debate. They prided themselves on being able to live in undesirable locations and to eat things that other groups considered inedible such as snakes, cacti, spiders, etc. When they settled in the middle of Lake Texcoco on the island of Tenochtitlán, they began an advanced system of hydroponics—or floating gardens—called *chinampas*. They literally created more land around the island by pounding massive poles into the lake bed and then filling in the space with earth, creating garden plots that did not need to be watered. In this way they expanded the cultivable area around the island on the lake bottom, and grew a variety of agricultural products including corn, beans, squash, chili peppers, tomatoes, avocados, and other things. They also utilized the lake for its fish and water fowl. Finally, the Aztecs practiced anthropophagi, or cannibalism, perhaps to a greater degree than any other civilization in world history—more on this below.

Like the Maya, Aztec society was very stratified. However, unlike the Maya, the Aztecs had a single universal emperor called the *Tlatoani*. This individual was considered a deity, and very strict rules existed regarding the manner in which subjects could interact with him. For example, making eye contact with the *Tlatoani* was forbidden, as was touching him. The Spanish chroniclers alleged that the Aztec emperor ate human flesh every day as part of his regular diet.

Below the emperor was the nobility, who aided the *Tlatoani* in running the affairs of the empire. The nobility consisted of governors of various levels of the political bureaucracy, priests (who will be discussed below), and warriors. Warriors were particularly important in Aztec society, and as minor nobles they enjoyed many privileges in society that others did not. In fact, the Aztec military had various different warrior societies such as the Jaguar Warriors and Eagle Warriors who were among the elite in the Aztec fighting machine. Warriors were the vehicle whereby conquests took place and through which tribute payments were made.

The next level in Aztec social hierarchy was that of the commoners. Individuals such as small landowners, craftsmen, artisans, and other minor citizens were among this group. Below the common citizens were the peasants. These lowest of the social classes were not usually landowners, but were farm laborers who grew and gathered food for the empire. They were animal tenders, hunters, and farmers. In addition to their responsibilities as food producers, they also provided manual labor that was necessary for the construction of the massive temples and palaces that were built on the island city of Tenochtitlán. Finally, the peasantry was also frequently used as sacrificial victims in the Aztec religious ceremonies. Because the Aztecs practiced human sacrifice on such an unprecedented scale, they were always in need of humans to send to the sacrificial altars. And while some of these victims were captives taken on the battlefield, most were peasants from surrounding villages and conquered tributary groups.

Aztec religion was brutal, bloodthirsty, and violent. Religion was the most important day-to-day motivation for most of the activities in Aztec society. In fact, in the Aztec calendar, every day of the calendar year except for five days at the end of the year, was designated as a period of sacrifice for a specific deity and precise details were to be followed. For example, during the festival of *Tozoztontli*, honoring the god Tlaloc, crops were planted and captives were flayed alive. Another festival for the god Quetzalcoatl involved the sacrificing of children. Sacrificial days designated for the primary deity Huitzilopochtli involved massive numbers of victims who had their hearts removed from their chest cavities in ritual heart sacrifice.

Like the Maya, the Aztecs did practice auto-sacrifice or bloodletting. But the difference was that, unlike the Maya, the Aztecs did not view bloodletting as the primary means of appeasing the gods. Instead, auto-sacrifice was performed as an alternative to heart sacrifice, which was the pinnacle of religious worship. Furthermore, some forms of Aztec auto-sacrifice involved not just the practice of spilling one's own blood from ear lobe, tongue, or penis, but could also involve ritualistic suicide as well.

Heart sacrifice was performed frequently by Aztec priests. The victim was laid over a rounded stone altar, his limbs were held, and his beating heart was cut out of his chest with a sharp obsidian knife. The hearts and blood were kept in bowls in Aztec temples, and often heads were displayed on skull racks. The bodies were unceremoniously toppled down the pyramid steps, and often the fleck was carried away and prepared as food for certain individuals and occasions. Author R.C. Padden describes the particularly bloody scene at a temple dedication in Tenochtitlán in this way:

> The lambs were slaughtered with machine-like precision; it took but seconds to dispatch each victim. Rivulets of blood became bright streams; the freshets became rivers of blood, gradually breaking off huge clotted chunks and carrying them down stream as though in height of springtime flood. At the pyramid's base priests wallowed and skidded about as they removed the bodies and hearts by the ton. Others bailed up blood in jars and cups. The holocaust went on unabated for four days and nights. Most sources claim that over 80000 were sacrificed during those incredible 96 hours. The stench grew so overpowering, the revulsion so general, that there was an exodus from the city.
>
> *(Padden 1970: 73)*

Scholars have attempted to articulate the rationale behind Aztec actions and religious ceremonies. The religious answer to the question of why the Aztecs performed such bloody and violent ceremonies was simply that it was required by their gods and deities. Others have attempted to argue that the practices of human sacrifice and cannibalism were performed to make up for a protein deficiency in the Aztec diet. But this does not seem likely given the fact that the Aztecs did have protein in their diet from fish, birds, dogs, and other animals. The most accepted theory is a political one. Aztec actions seem to have been a demonstration of their awesome power over their people and subjected tributaries. As an act of calculated terror, human sacrifice would have sent a strong political message to conquered tribes and unconquered enemies of the political and military might of the powerful Aztec governmental system.

When the Spanish arrived in Tenochtitlán in 1519, they were appalled by what they saw, and soon they proceeded to destroy the Aztec civilization out of a systematic and religiously dogmatic view of their beliefs, but also out of horror at the behavior of Aztec priests and nobles. The Spanish viewed Aztec beliefs and practices as summarily Satanic and proceeded to eradicate them as quickly and efficiently as possible.

The Inca

Finally we come to the Inca of the Peruvian highlands. In the 1500s, they became the largest—in terms of geography—and most complex empire in the Western Hemisphere. By 1438, the Inca began a series of conquests of groups near their ceremonial capital city, Cuzco. Over the next century they grew to their furthest extent, reaching from modern-day Ecuador in the north, to northern Chile in the south. They maintained their control over the regional inhabitants through state-sponsored use of language (the official language of the Inca Empire was Quechua), a state religion, forced resettlement, and forced labor systems. Finally, the Inca developed a curious writing and tallying system called the *quipu*, a bundle of knotted cords of different lengths and colors, whereby they could keep track of commodities and record information.

Feeding such a large empire was challenging, and becomes mind-boggling when we consider that the empire stretched from the coastal regions of the Andes mountains, all the way to the summit of the mountains themselves, reaching elevations of nearly 8000 feet above sea level. In order to farm on the sides of mountains, the Inca resorted to intensive terracing, fertilization, and irrigation. The principal staple crop was potatoes, but others were cultivated such as beans, corn, and other vegetables. They farmed different crops at different elevations up the sides of the mountains so that they could produce a variety of edible plants, even if these plants grew in differing conditions, temperatures, altitudes, and so forth. Then, through a system of vertical reciprocity, they redistributed the goods they produced up and down the mountains so that communities at differing elevations could consume some of what was produced at all the different elevations. Finally, the Inca also developed a method for preserving potatoes and meat by freeze-drying the food. Potatoes were set out on the ground in huge parcels, and then workers would step on them in order to press the moisture out of the potatoes. Then, they would freeze at night, and the process was repeated for several days until the result was a preserved potato (called *chuño*) that could be stored for future use.

Inca society was also very interesting. Like the Aztecs, the Inca were a monarchical empire with an emperor at the top. The Inca emperor—whose title was simply the Inca—was a political and religious ruler and quasi deity. Below the emperor was a group of territorial rulers and nobles who governed various districts within the empire. Some of the districts were quite large, overseeing literally tens of thousands of individuals, while others were small, encompassing no more than a few villages. The bulk of the population of the Inca Empire was made of up the lower-class peasantry who were organized in clans called *ayllu*. Within an *ayllu*, the people were responsible for the taxes that were paid to the empire. But the tax in the Inca system was not a commodity-based tax. Rather, the Inca were taxed in a system of labor-tax called *mita*. Usually the way this worked was that in each community a plot of ground was set aside for the political/religious leaders of the empire at the various levels of political power. The people in the *ayllu* would work this special plot of ground right along with their own land, including plowing, planting, fertilizing, harvesting, and so forth. Then, when the land was harvested, the produce from the government's plot of land was sent up to the governors and regional leaders and religious figures in order to sustain them in their positions. The rest of the produce from a clan's land was used by the clan as needed. Other forms of *mita* tax included military service for males, and cloth production for females.

In terms of Inca religion, the Inca were highly polytheistic, like the Maya and Aztecs. Their deities were predominantly nature gods and goddesses, under the authority of a supreme god named Viracocha. Other ancestor gods and even clan deities were also worshipped and presented with offerings of gold, precious stones, animals, and food. These offerings were often kept in special temple-structures called *huacas*. Some of the hemisphere's greatest metallurgy in gold and silver was produced by Inca gold- and silversmiths who crafted these metals into intricate works of art that are still celebrated to this day. Finally, the Inca did practice human sacrifice, but not on the same scale as the Maya or Aztecs. Often, the individuals who were sacrificed were mummified and left in *huacas* or in high mountain passes as offerings for the gods. The Inca also sacrificed llamas and other animals.

Filmography

Films depicting pre-Columbian Indian cultures in Latin America are rare. Usually the only portrayals of native cultures come associated with the baggage of Spanish contact. Rarely have filmmakers presented movies about unadulterated Indian cultures in Latin America prior to European contact. One of the recent exceptions to this situation is the film *Apocalypto* (2006) by Mel Gibson. And while the film is not without its problems, it remains one of the few attempts by filmmakers to render native Latin American cultures prior to the changes that were brought to Indian civilizations by contact with the Spanish and Portuguese.

Apocalypto *(2006)*

Mel Gibson's film *Apocalypto* is visually stunning and fast-paced. It was filmed in the Yucatec Mayan language, which lends a level of authenticity to the production. And it was filmed on location in Veracruz, Mexico, and El Petén, Guatemala, which provided a sense of realism that could not be accomplished in a studio. Having said all this, the film is also quirky in some ways from a historical and archaeological perspective, which detracts from the film as a whole.

The movie opens on a hunting scene where a tapir is pursued by Mayan hunters. This scene is reflective of the positive and negative elements throughout the rest of the film. The hunters pursue the wild pig with primitive weapons, wearing little because of the climate and environment of the jungle where they live. The hunters are tattooed, scarred, and pierced in ways that resemble what scholars have authenticated about the ancient Maya civilization. Their dress and hairstyles are similar to those found in ancient Mayan inscriptions and vase paintings. All of these features lend a feeling of accuracy and authenticity to the film. But then, as the hunt reaches climax, the pig is trapped by a series of nets and then pierced through by a Rambo-style booby-trap that the hunters have created and set for the purpose of catching the tapir. The nets and spikes that impale the pig spring up from the ground as if by magic, which diminishes the feeling of authenticity that the film has been nurturing to this point. It is likely that Maya hunters did use spears and nets to catch their prey, but the way this is portrayed in the film seems to be overly dramatic. As the hunt comes to an end, the hunters meet a wandering band of Maya who have been driven from their homes. This encounter sets up the conflict for the film; the wanderers tell of a coming scourge that will soon overtake the land.

The hunters return to their village and spend the evening listening to stories told by the village elders. The next morning in the early dawn hours, while the people are quiet and asleep, the village is suddenly attacked by another group of Maya warriors whose appearance is so disparate from those of the village that they seem to be an entirely different kind of people. They dress more elaborately, with more bodily ornamentation and costume jewelry. They are also tattooed and scarred with scarification techniques. But their bodily ornamentation is much more ornate than that of the poorer central villagers. As the villagers fight with these enemy warriors, much of the village is burned and many people are carried away as captives. The main protagonist, Jaguar Paw (Rudy Youngblood), is also captured along with several other men from the village.

After an arduous journey, the captives arrive in a large Maya city that resembles some of the famous Maya ruins in Mexico and Guatemala, most specifically the site of Tikal in the Guatemalan Highlands, and Chichén Itza in Mexico's Yucatan Peninsula. This scene is very accurately recreated. Slaves work to burn limestone in order to cover the pyramids and temples with white plaster. The captives walk past corn fields where corn, squash, and other crops are tended. Turkeys are seen in the markets as well as iguana, jaguars, and other animals. Women weave and dye cloth and it is apparent that Gibson paid special attention to detail in the construction of this set. As the prisoners of war are guided through the city, women come out and slather them with blue paint, signifying their status as captives and sacrificial victims. This is also very accurate based on both Maya paintings and central Mexican codices. Finally, the citizens of this Maya city are much wealthier than the villagers we are familiar with. In addition to the body scarification, tattoos, and piercings mentioned above, they also have teeth that have been filed to points and filled with jade and other precious stones. They wear a lot of jade ornamentation on their faces and bodies. And, some of the royalty are decked out in brilliant red and green feathers, the latter of which come from the quetzal bird of Guatemala.

The captives are eventually brought to the base of an enormous pyramid. The front steps are drenched in blood and the priests at the top of the temple drop heads down the stairs where they are caught and placed on pikes throughout the city. Jaguar Paw and the other captives are directed to the top of the pyramid where they are also to be sacrificed. The priests at the top of the temple stand in the company of the royalty of the Maya city. One of these leaders speaks of restoring order to the cosmos through heart sacrifice. He says that they are sacrificing their victims to Kululkán, the Maya version of the Central Mexican and Aztec deity Quetzalcoatl. The first captive in line is bent over a stone altar back down and his four limbs are held while a priest raises a ceremonial knife and plunges it into his chest. The priest then reaches into the man's chest cavity and rips out his beating heart. After showing the beating heart to the sacrificial victim, it is placed on a brazier of hot coals and taken away. The victim's body is then decapitated, and the head and body are tossed unceremoniously from the top of the pyramid.

This episode of human sacrifice is the most controversial element of Gibson's film. While it is certain that the Maya did practice human sacrifice, and also that they did use captives for this purpose from time to time, they were more likely to practice auto-sacrifice or bloodletting. The form of heart sacrifice that Gibson portrays in his film, with all its grisly gore, was the primary method of human sacrifice in the Aztec Empire, not the Maya. The Aztecs practiced human sacrifice on a daily basis and much of this was carried out through the ceremonial removing of hearts from bodies. Gibson seems to have been faced with the option of depicting bloodletting or something more dramatic, and instead of portraying a Maya priest in a bloodletting ceremony, Gibson opted to show Aztec rites as an alternative.

When it is Jaguar Paw's turn to be sacrificed, a full solar eclipse of the sun saves his life and the rest of the captives are taken somewhere else to be killed.

FIGURE 2.1 *Apocalypto* (2006, Touchstone Pictures).

This is probably not a very accurate portrayal of the treatment of captives. After all the work the Maya warriors went through to get the captives, they would likely have kept them alive for a future sacrificial episode. As the warriors attempt to kill him, Jaguar Paw manages to escape into the jungle, pursued by Maya warriors. These warriors use accurately portrayed weapons such as bows and arrows, spear throwers, and Aztec-style *macuahuitl*, a wooden club with bits of sharp obsidian embedded into the sides to form a sword-like weapon. When the Maya warriors become angry at their inability to capture Jaguar Paw, they swear that they will catch him, flay him, eat him, and wear his skin. Once again Gibson relies on the Aztecs for material instead of the Maya; this particular practice of wearing the flayed skin of a captive was practiced by Aztec priests.

Finally, after much running through the jungle, protracted chase scenes, and more Rambo-style traps, Jaguar Paw and his pursuers reach the sea where they see four ships flying Spanish flags. Apparently, they are viewing the ships and crew of Christopher Columbus on his fourth voyage, when he reached the mainland of Central America. There does exist an account of Columbus interacting with a group of Maya off the coast of Central America, and this is apparently what Gibson is attempting to portray. But instead of filming any interaction between the Maya and the Spanish, Jaguar Paw and the other surviving Maya villagers retreat back into the jungle to begin a new life.

Conclusions

Mel Gibson's *Apocalypto* is valuable as a filmographic document because it presents a vivid image of life in ancient Mesoamerica. It portrays the lifestyle, religion, society, and cultural awareness of the Maya and other groups. It also depicts the fierce independence and warlike tendencies that some Maya societies upheld during the Classic Period. But Gibson's work is also flawed in many ways that may not detract from the historical setting for viewers who are not concerned about accuracies, but that do present an inaccurate illustration for those who are seeking for a truer portrayal of the ancient Maya.

In Mexico, reactions to the film were varied. In a critique of the film in the *Los Angeles Times*, Bartolome Alonzo Caamal, a Maya language teacher in Yucatan, said the film spent too much time depicting violence and not enough time demonstrating Maya accomplishments in writing, science, and math. In the same article, Juan Tiney, a member of Guatemala's Indian and Farmer Coordinating Council, said: "The level of violence in the film could lead some to say the Mayas were a violent people who could only be saved by the arrival of the Spanish, when history shows it was quite the opposite." Maya specialists in the United States also took issue with Gibson's depiction of Aztec practices in a Maya film. In Austin's *American Statesman*, art history professor Julia Guernsey said, "I think Mel Gibson is the worst thing that's happened to indigenous populations since the arrival of the Spanish."

Further Reading

Coe, Michael D. *Mexico*. London: Thames & Hudson, 2008.
Coe, Michael D. *The Maya*. London: Thames & Hudson, 2011.
Moseley, Michael E. *The Incas and Their Ancestors*. London: Thames & Hudson, 2001.
Padden, R.C. *The Hummingbird and the Hawk*. New York: HarperCollins, 1970.
Smith, Michael E. *The Aztecs*. Oxford: Wiley-Blackwell, 2012.

3

THE GREAT ENCOUNTER—THE ENIGMA OF CHRISTOPHER COLUMBUS

Since I know that you will be pleased at the great success with which the Lord has crowned my voyage, I write to inform you how in thirty-three days I crossed from the Canary Islands to the Indies, with the fleet which our most illustrious sovereigns gave me. I found very many islands with large populations and took possession of them all for their Highnesses; this I did by proclamation and unfurled the royal standard. No opposition was offered.

Christopher Columbus

Introduction

The year 1992 was both hailed and reviled around the world as the 500th anniversary of the arrival of Christopher Columbus in the Americas. Columbus was certainly not the first European explorer to journey to the New World, but he was one of the most important simply because of the fact that the Spanish kingdom of Castile—the territory that bankrolled his 1492 expedition—had the financial means and religious zeal to follow up his initial encounter with thousands of settlers, missionaries, and soldiers in the years following 1492.

Columbus' voyage was also highly significant in terms of the history of Latin America. Prior to European contact with the Amerindian civilizations of the New World, Native American historical sources such as stone monuments, bark-paper books, knotted cords, oral traditions, and architecture all existed in the New World. But these sources present special challenges in terms of their physical longevity, and also in the difficulties Europeans faced in understanding the content of these sources. In addition, the historical records of the American Indian civilizations were prized by scholars and historians, and despised by priests who viewed many such documents as the work of the devil, deserving physical destruction. But in either case, they proved difficult, and in some cases, impossible to decipher.

However, over the course of the sixteenth century, as Spanish chroniclers such as Christopher Columbus, Bernal Díaz del Castillo, Bartolomé de las Casas, and others wrote down their observations and experiences in the New World, a history of Latin America began to grow and develop, and much of the documentation was preserved in European repositories such as the great Casa de Contratación in Seville, which serves as one of the largest archives of colonial Latin American documents in the world today. Because of the difficulties of capturing indigenous history prior to the conquest in ways Europeans could understand, the early history of Latin America became predominantly a product of the Spanish language of the conquerors and settlers from Spain. Indian languages and dialects continued to be used by the Native Americans, but they were slowly replaced by Spanish as a *lingua franca* throughout most of the hemisphere. At first this was problematic because the documents that were written by soldiers, priests, and others were very one-sided in perspective—Spaniards writing in Spanish about themselves and their perceptions of the Indian civilizations they interacted with. Eventually, however, Indian perspectives were also recorded, either by Indians themselves who learned Spanish, or by priests who learned to speak the native languages, and who could translate Indian accounts into Spanish.

The voyages of Christopher Columbus (Columbus sailed to the New World four times between 1492 and 1504) provide scholars with some of the earliest historical documents to relate the tale of this contact between Europe and America. Columbus' initial voyage in 1492 opened the door for a massive flood of European settlement into the New World by Spain and eventually Portugal and other European nations as well. The Iberian explorers encountered numerous civilizations in the Americas that were both amazing and repugnant to their European sensibilities. American Indians had constructed impressive pyramids and seemingly floating cities, while also practicing human sacrifice and cannibalism. Perhaps at no other time in modern history was the contact between cultures so dramatic and charged with meaning.

Precursors and Problems

Christopher Columbus, as both man and legend, is equally fascinating and bewildering. He was monomaniacal at times in his zeal to sail west in search of Asian trade. Historians are occasionally hesitant to bestow too much emphasis on the achievements and actions of single individuals, but it is also intriguing to contemplate the vast and lasting effect that certain individuals can have on the world around them. Columbus was such a man.

As early as 1476, Columbus began to contemplate the spice and silk trade that existed between Europe and Asia. His residence in Portugal at that time placed him in a unique position to benefit from some of the most advanced navigational and cartographical knowledge in Europe. Portugal's Crown Prince Henry had established a seafaring school in Portugal in 1419, and by 1441 Portuguese ships had sailed the north Atlantic coast of Africa looking for gold, ivory, and other lucrative trade items. In 1487 a Portuguese navigator named Bartolomeu Dias reached the Cape of Good Hope at the southern-most tip of Africa, and in 1497, just five years after Columbus made his first legendary voyage to the Americas, Vasco da Gama reached India, where he traded for spices that brought extraordinary monetary wealth to Portugal.

By 1484, Columbus had developed the rudiments of his plan to sail west in order to reach the East. He posited that the Atlantic Ocean was much smaller, and that the Asian landmass was much larger, than contemporary scholars believed, thus making his proposed journey at least arguable. However, in 1484 when he requested money from King João II of Portugal for his voyage, he was denied on the basis that his numbers were very likely inaccurate, and that he and his crew would certainly starve to death in the vast ocean sea. It is important to note that by the end of the fifteenth century, there was really no question among the more sophisticated cultures of Europe that the earth was in fact a globe, so the old notion that the European powers were reticent to fund Columbus because of the danger of his falling off the edge of a flat earth should be laid to rest. There were in reality two primary obstacles that Columbus needed to defeat in order to succeed in his proposed venture of sailing west in order to arrive in Asia, and it was these two obstacles that persuaded the king of Portugal to withhold funding for the project. The first was the cost of the venture, a cost that forced Columbus to seek royal benefactors to fund his efforts. The second was the fact that, even though Columbus did not run the risk of falling off the earth, there was the very real possibility that he and his crew would all starve to death before they arrived at their destination because they would not be able to carry large enough quantities of food and fresh water to cross the vast oceanic distance.

So with King João's refusal of funding, Columbus abandoned Portugal and traveled to Spain in 1485 where he was soon introduced to Isabella I, queen of the Spanish kingdoms of Castile and Leon, and to her husband Ferdinand II, king of the Spanish kingdom of Aragon (the small Spanish kingdoms would not be united under one monarch until Isabella and Ferdinand's grandson Carlos—later known as Charles I—became king of Spain in 1516). Columbus' goal in traveling to Spain was to obtain royal funding for his anticipated voyage. But as in Portugal, his request was also denied by Queen Isabella on the grounds that she was fighting a war against the Spanish-Muslims from North Africa who had occupied the Iberian Peninsula for more than 700 years, since 711AD, and she needed all her funds for that war. Columbus was obliged to wait nearly seven years, until 1492, before the queen would entertain his proposal again.

And so we come to the year 1492, an exceptionally important year for several reasons, not least of which being that this was the year that Columbus "sailed the ocean blue." However, other events transpired earlier in the year that were equally important. In January 1492, Queen Isabella and her armies finally conquered the last Muslim stronghold in Iberia, the southern city of Granada. Later, in March 1492, Isabella decreed that all Jews in Spain would either convert to Roman Catholicism or face expulsion from the kingdoms of Spain. Finally, in August 1492, Columbus set sail toward the west and the unknown New World.

After Isabella drove the Muslims from Granada, Columbus approached her again to request funding for his voyage to the rich spice-lands of Asia. Her advisors, while not as knowledgeable about seafaring and navigation as those of the Portuguese Crown, nevertheless advised her against funding Columbus. Why she went against the counsel of her advisors is debatable, but she eventually granted funds and ships to Columbus for his voyage. In addition to the ships, Queen Isabella and Christopher Columbus entered into a contract of sorts, at Columbus' instigation, wherein she agreed to grant him titles of nobility, the office of Admiral of the Ocean Sea, 10 percent of the wealth generated for Spain, the right to governorship over any lands he discovered, and all of these remunerations would be his in perpetuity and inheritable by his posterity forever.

The question as to why Columbus needed financial support is not difficult to understand owing to the length of the proposed journey, and the fact that he had very little in terms of liquid assets of his own. But the more compelling question remains, why did Columbus repeatedly make such financial requests of European royalty—his requests had been laid before the monarchs of Portugal and Spain, and he even sent family members to the royal courts of France and England begging support—instead of seeking financial backing from other fiscal entities or money-lenders? The answer must lay in the fact that Columbus did not only seek for funding for the voyages, but also for the titles of nobility, admiralty, and governorship, all inheritable to his posterity forever. While a private investor could have funded his proposed voyage, only a monarch could have granted him his other desires.

On the other hand, scholars have also entertained the issue of Isabella's concurrence in Columbus' demands. Why would a monarch of a powerful European country agree to Columbus' outlandish expectations of nobility, wealth, and political power? Perhaps the answer may be found in the fact that if Columbus failed to return from his first voyage, Isabella would not have lost too much in terms of assets; after all, she did not—as is sometimes related—have to sell off her crown jewels to finance his journey. However, if Columbus did in fact return from the East with wealth in the form of spices, silks, gold, and ivory, Spain would gain more wealth and power in Europe, which would offset any contractual obligations between Columbus and the Spanish Crown.

Columbus' First Voyage

So, with the contractual arrangements worked out, Columbus left Spain on August 3, 1492, heading southwest toward the Canary Islands off the northwest coast of Africa, where he finished outfitting the ships, his crew, and their supplies. On September 8, 1492, Columbus, 90 men, and three ships departed from the Canary Islands and sailed west into the Atlantic Ocean. The historical records of this first journey across the ocean sea were kept by Columbus himself. Unfortunately, what is left of the ship's logs are somewhat unreliable. Ship captains were obliged to keep an official log of their progress, the things they saw, and the details of their voyages. One of the key elements of a ship's log was the distance traveled every day.

In Columbus' case, he actually kept two logs, a public log and a secret log, the latter of which was the more accurate in terms of distance sailed. Why the subterfuge? Columbus knew, as did his crew, that the ships carried a finite amount of fresh water and food. And, at a specific distance away from the Canary Islands, they would cross the proverbial point of no return, where they would have consumed half of their supplies and would have to either turn back or face the very real threat of starvation. So the public log reported a distance that was less than the distance recorded in the secret log. In this way, Columbus gambled with his life and the lives of his crew, and by the time they discovered the deception, they had already lost the opportunity to make it safely back to the Canary Islands. When mutiny became a very real possibility, Columbus used his skills as an orator to talk his crew into trusting him, and they ultimately changed their minds about tossing him from the boat.

The complete journey took just over 30 days. Land was sighted somewhere in the Bahamas on October 12, 1492. Columbus named the island they landed upon San Salvador, and claimed it for Isabella, queen of Castile. Modern scholars disagree about the exact location of Columbus' San Salvador, but agree that it was in the Bahamas, east of Florida and northeast of Cuba. Columbus and his men briefly interacted with the native inhabitants of the island, probably Arawak or Taino Indians, and then returned to the sea to continue searching for the wealth of the Indies. By the end of the month of October, Columbus had sailed southwest until he sighted the island of Cuba.

Following a short-lived exploration of a small portion of the northern coast, he sailed east and sighted the island of Hispaniola early in December. While exploring the northern coast of the island, one of his ships, the *Santa María*, hit a coral reef and sank. This was particularly bad news because the *Santa María* had been the largest of Columbus' ships and carried a crew of around 40 men. Now that the ship was damaged beyond repair, there was not enough space on the other two vessels to carry the crew of the *Santa María* back to Spain. So, some of the timber from the *Santa María* was salvaged and used to construct a rude shelter on the northern coast of Hispaniola. Columbus named the settlement Navidad, because of the fact that the *Santa María* sank on Christmas Day, and designated 39 men to remain behind and await his return when he would rescue them and return them to Spain. Then, Columbus commandeered the *Niña* for as his personal ship for the voyage home.

While in the Caribbean, Columbus and his men interacted with several different Indian groups. Some of the information from these encounters has survived in the letters and logbooks of Columbus and others. Columbus records:

> It seemed to me that they were a people very poor in everything. They were very well formed, with handsome bodies and good faces. Their hair is coarse—almost like the tail of a horse—and short. They wear their hair down over their eyebrows except for a little in the back which they wear long and never cut. Some of them paint themselves with black, and some of them with red, and some of them with whatever they find. They are the color of the Canarians, neither black nor white. And some of them paint their faces, and some of them only the eyes, and some of them only the nose. They do not carry arms nor are they acquainted with them because I showed them swords and they took them by the edge and through ignorance cut themselves. They have no iron. Their javelins are shafts without iron and some of them have at the end a fish tooth and other of other things. All of them alike are of good-sized stature and carry themselves well. I have not found the human monsters which many people expected.[1]

It seems clear that Columbus was interested in these newly discovered peoples and was determined to express his interest to the Crown and the nobles in Castile and the other provinces of Spain. He further described the Indians in these words:

> I saw some who had marks of wounds on their bodies and I made signs to them asking what they were; and they showed me how people from other islands nearby came there and tried to take them, and how they defended themselves . . . To the east is a land called Bohio which they said was very large and that there were people on it who had one eye in their foreheads, and others whom they called cannibals, of whom they showed great fear . . . because the cannibals eat them, and that they are people very well armed. Since they are armed they must be people of intelligence.[2]

And finally:

> They should be very good and intelligent servants, for I see that they say very quickly everything that is said to them; and I believe that they would

become Christians very easily, for it seemed to me that they had no religion. Our Lord pleasing, at the time of my departure I will take six of
them from here to Your Highness in order that they may learn to speak.[3]

It seems clear that Columbus and those who traveled with him had many mis-
conceptions about the Native American cultures they encountered on the island
of Hispaniola, and they made several judgments that clearly delineate their preju-
dices and superior notions of themselves and Iberian culture in general.

Conclusions

Columbus returned to Spain on March 15, 1493. Columbus' first voyage was
the stuff of legends, and he returned to Spain to a hero's welcome. He brought
with him Native American Indians and some gold trinkets that had been confiscated from the Caribbean tribes. This first voyage sparked Spain's interest in
the New World, the possibility of long-distance trade, and the prospect of
evangelization among an entirely unknown population of American Indians.
Columbus quickly outfitted a second voyage and set sail for the Americas on
September 24, 1493 with nearly 20 ships and around 1200 men. In all, Columbus
crossed the Atlantic Ocean eight times in four separate voyages, preparing the
way for a flood of new explorations and conquest in the New World. Lastly,
while Christopher Columbus was certainly not the first individual or even
European to reach the American Hemisphere, he did survive the return voyage
(which many before him did not accomplish) and opened the doors to the Age
of Imperialism.

Filmography

The voyages of Christopher Columbus have been depicted for film, television,
and even animation. Three films will be reviewed here; *Christopher Columbus*
(1949) is the oldest, and both *Christopher Columbus: The Discovery* (1992) and
1492: Conquest of Paradise (1992) were produced and released in conjunction
with the 500th anniversary of Columbus' initial 1492 voyage. Each of the three
has merit and positive attributes, but each film is also flawed in some fundamental
way that requires historians to take issue with the portrayal. Of the three, *1492*
is arguably the most ambitious in scope and presentation, and also the most
controversial in terms of discrepancies with the historical record.

In addition, the two films released in 1992 were produced to both celebrate
and vilify Columbus and his accomplishment in 1492. As recently as the mid-
1970s, many Native Americans have begun to be highly critical of Columbus
and his commemoration on the American holiday of Columbus Day. They
argue that Columbus represents the beginning of the destruction of Native
American culture in the New World, through forced migration, enslavement,

and the introduction of European diseases such as smallpox that the native Indians had no immunities for and that caused the deaths of millions of Native Americans. In many locations in the United States, the second Monday of October has been renamed Indigenous Peoples' Day to celebrate the native cultures of the Americas that were wiped out by Europeans following Columbus' first crossing.

Christopher Columbus *(1949)*

In 1949, following World War II and just prior to the Korean conflict, director David MacDonald released the film titled simply *Christopher Columbus* (1949). The film was an attempt to entertain the American population with a story of adventure and timely discovery, at a time when the nation needed encouragement and relief from conflict. *Columbus* portrays the man Christopher Columbus as a driven, manipulative man who would stop at nothing to achieve his goals. The film begins in 1485 in a Spanish monastery. Columbus says that he is in Spain to ask the queen for permission and funds for the fateful voyage. He argues to those around him that he wants to sail to India to convert heathens and get gold, even though the lucrative trade in India was in tea and spices, not gold.

Soon, however, the film goes astray as Columbus states that he wants to find a new world across the ocean. In actual fact, Columbus did not intend to find a new world; he desired to get to Asia where the profitable spice trade was located. When he finally gets an audience with Queen Isabella, he is dismissed by King Ferdinand, which is likely inaccurate because his negotiations were with the queen alone. He tells the queen that in Portugal they know very little about sailing and the Atlantic Ocean, which is obviously incorrect.

When Columbus presents his ideas to the queen's council in the film, he makes several mistakes, including reminding them that the world is round and talk about new lands between Europe and Asia in the Atlantic Ocean. After Columbus is rejected and prepares to leave Spain for France, Isabella is told that the voyage he proposes would be too costly, whereupon she attempts to sell her riches to fund the journey, which is ridiculous and a story that should be laid to rest once and for all. Columbus is eventually called back before the queen and given three ships and the blessing of the Church. The film does not indicate where the ships came from or how Isabella came to her decision to fund his expedition.

On the expedition, the historical personality Diego de Arana serves as a character for Columbus to confide in as a way of getting information to the viewer. For example, Columbus mentions to Arana that he is keeping two log books, one that is accurate and one that is not. Interestingly, the *Santa María* is depicted with a needle compass, which was inaccurate since this kind of compass for maritime exploration was not introduced in Europe until the early 1800s. Later on, during the expedition, the crew begins to grumble about the voyage; not that they are going to fall off of a flat earth, but that they are going to run out of food before they arrive at their destination, a point that *is* quite accurate.

Eventually, a mutiny begins and includes much swordplay and knife-throwing. Columbus talks the mutineers down and promises that if they don't find land within three days they will turn around and sail home, which would have been impossible at that point due to the lack of supplies and fresh water on the ships by then. Soon, they sight birds and branches in the water, indicating that they are near land. Columbus sights land first and they go ashore where they pray in thanksgiving for their safe arrival.

Not long after landfall, native Indians appear and approach the Spaniards en masse. One of the Indians comes forward and kneels on the ground placing his spear before the Spanish. This is purely ridiculous, as is the fact that the Spanish have very little trouble talking to and understanding the Indians. Columbus pronounces that they are there to convert the Indians, not steal from them, whereupon he steals something from one of his own soldiers to use to barter for a piece of gold with one of the Indians.

To the film's credit, it does depict the *Santa María* running around and sinking on Christmas Eve. The salvage is brought ashore and Columbus decides to leave 40 men behind to explore and preach to the Indians. Then Columbus returns to Spain where he is brought before the monarchs, who he presents with gifts of gold and talking birds who say things like "Long live the Queen."

The film concludes with the treatment of Columbus several years after his first voyage. The court and the Crown have turned against him and agree that he is a poor governor of the lands across the ocean. In the New World, Columbus is accused of several infractions and put in chains. Onboard the ship, the captain offers to remove the chains but Columbus refuses saying he will wear the chains until he is granted an audience with the queen. The film ends with a soliloquy by Columbus stating that long after he is dead, future generations will remember him.

In October 1949, Bosley Crowther reviewed the film for the *New York Times*. He points out that the film was the latest attempt by British filmmakers to break into the American market. He remarks that the film "is largely an uninspired succession of legendary but lifeless episode[s]" taken from the pages of history. Indeed, Crowther's only real praise for the film is in the portrayal of authentic costumes and colorful reproductions of palaces and ships. However, the rest of the film is "so heavily weighted with dramaless pageantry that the customer, like Columbus, is prey to tedium e'er the ships even put to sea."

Christopher Columbus: The Discovery *(1992)*

Christopher Columbus: The Discovery (1992) was directed by John Glen and released in 1992 on the quincentenary of Columbus' landing in the New World. This film boasts a cast of all-stars (Marlon Brando, Tom Selleck, Catherine

Zeta-Jones) or soon-to-be stars (Benicio del Toro, Manuel de Blas, Peter Guinness), but in some cases this does not benefit the film's presentation. The film is fairly lighthearted and leans toward the ridiculous on some occasions. Columbus is portrayed as a young man, who is carefree and dashing. At the beginning of the film, he has a fight with some Muslims who are portrayed to be less intelligent that Columbus, and easily defeated. Columbus, played by Georges Corraface, is then shown in a monastery where he and his son Diego have lived for some time while they wait for a decision from Queen Isabella. While in the monastery, Columbus speaks with the priests about whether or not the world is round, a typical mistake made by filmmakers who desire to incorporate this old notion (that Europeans still thought the world was flat) into their films about Columbus.

After a short time, Columbus is permitted to attend Queen Isabella and King Ferdinand at court, where he presents his idea of sailing west to reach the East Indies. After some negotiation, his proposal is accepted and a contract is drawn up. These negotiations depicted in the film are incredibly simple and underdeveloped. When he discusses the voyage with the monarchs, he alludes to the fact that his voyage would be a perfect opportunity to preach the gospel in the Indies, playing upon the attitudes at the time of zealously spreading Christianity to combat the presence of Islam in Spain and other parts of the world. Finally, it is odd to see King Ferdinand (played by Tom Selleck) portrayed in such an active role in the negotiations; Queen Isabella was the primary monarch in the arbitrations since her realm of Castile bordered on Portugal and the Atlantic Ocean while Ferdinand's was oriented more toward the Mediterranean Sea. Perhaps the director felt that portraying a woman in the deal was less appealing than for two men to make a deal of such magnitude.

A Spaniard named Diego de Arana—the same historical figure mentioned above in *Christopher Columbus* (1949)—agrees to sail with Columbus to the Indies, and the film briefly develops the relationship between Columbus and Arana's sister Beatrice, who eventually bears Columbus a son. Eventually Columbus is taken to a dungeon where officials of the Spanish Inquisition torture individuals who are suspected of heresy. In an inexplicable exchange, Columbus is questioned by the Inquisitors and all but accused of being a heretic before finally being allowed to leave. The Spanish Inquisition was indeed active in Spain at this time, but there is no indication historically that Columbus was accused of heresy before his voyage.

Ultimately, Columbus' request to sail for Spain is denied based on the fact that the ocean is too large to cross. This is indeed accurate, and Columbus was forced to argue the distance of the ocean drawing upon the works of many ancient scholars and travelers who ventured to Asia and the Middle East. After the fall of the Muslim stronghold of Granada in southern Spain early in 1492, Columbus is again granted an audience with the monarchs in which Ferdinand again takes the lead in the discussion with Columbus, relegating Isabella to a secondary position—again, a situation that is historically inaccurate. Eventually Columbus is told to wait and granted a pension.

The film alludes to the 1492 order by Isabella that all Jews and Muslims in Castile must convert to Catholicism or leave Spain. Then, with little further discussion about why the monarchs changed their minds, Columbus is given ships and—in one of the most ridiculous scenes in the entire film—Isabella tells Columbus that she will pawn her crown jewels to fund his voyage; again, the director seems determined to include all of the old romantic, and historically inaccurate, notions about Columbus and his first voyage across the Ocean Sea. Columbus and Isabella enter into the famous contract wherein he asks for titles of nobility and executive power over new colonies, the admiralty of the Spanish Navy, and 10 percent of the wealth he would discover. The monarchs are frustrated that he asks for so much, but then decide that if he succeeds, the rewards would far surpass their current income and make his price worth the endeavor.

Director John Glen correctly brings Martín Alonso Pinzón into the film at this point; Pinzón was the owner of the ships and the captain of many of the crewmembers on Columbus' first voyage. The ships used for the filming were quite accurate and accentuated the realistic nature of the voyage. Unfortunately the acting and storyline get bogged down in minor trivial details with derail the overall portrayal. One such incident is the exposé of a saboteur on the ships who attempts to impair the voyage. This is a little odd and seems out of place with the historical facts regarding Columbus' crossing in 1492. Other oddities include the crew's fascination with a manta ray, and sharks eating a man who was thrown overboard, obviously an attempt to make the trip seem more exciting.

As in *Christopher Columbus* (1949), Glen includes the fact that Columbus kept two logbooks, one that accurately detailed the number of leagues they had traveled, and a fake book that depicted a shorter distance. The crew continues to grumble, however, and Columbus is constantly trying to assuage their fears. Finally, the crew threatens a mutiny and it is decided that in three days if they have not sighted land, they can cut off Columbus' head and return to Spain; again this threatened decapitation seems to have been included to add to the drama of the crossing. Unfortunately, as in the earlier film, they do not mention that it would have been impossible to return to Spain at that point of the voyage because the crew had already consumed more than half of the food and water on the ship.

On the third day, in a ridiculously contrived scene that serves only to make the journey more melodramatic, the crew prepares to cut off Columbus' head; then they all change their minds as a favorable wind picks up. Soon thereafter they sight land and all rejoice. The men of Columbus' crew go ashore and Columbus names the island San Salvador whereupon the men all sing a joyful song. As the men play games on the beach, Native Americans come out of the jungle. The Indians are portrayed as very accommodating. They have some gold ornaments that excite the Spaniards, and they show the Spaniards how to smoke tobacco in return for some of the crew's wine.

In a moment of true accuracy, Glen portrays the separation of Columbus and Pinzón as the latter takes the *Pinta* and sails off in search of more treasure. Pinzón eventually returns but the bad feelings between him and Columbus remain. On Christmas Eve, the *Santa María* runs aground and sinks. The crew salvages from the wreckage and then Columbus leaves some of the men behind including his friend Diego de Arana. Eventually, all of these men, including Arana would be killed by the natives, although the film depicts some of the men being crucified on crosses, which is terribly inaccurate. With the plundered gold and six Indians, Columbus boards the *Niña* and they sail for Spain in the two remaining ships. On the return voyage, Pinzón and Columbus are again separated, probably because the former desired to be the first to return to Spain and claim the glory for the expedition.

When Columbus arrives back in Spain, again as in the earlier film, he is greeted as a returning hero. He presents gold and Indians to the monarchs and he receives his titles of nobility, admiral, and viceroy of the Indies. Then, the film abruptly ends, leaving unanswered questions and historical fallacies about the voyage, the fate of Pinzón, and the future voyages that Columbus took across the Atlantic Ocean.

The film was plagued with problems from the start. Several of the actors who were cast in leading roles in the film backed out late in the planning stages, leaving director Glen to fill the roles at the last minute. Marlon Brando, who portrayed a representative of the Church and the court named Tomás de Torquemada, even attempted to have his name omitted from the film's credits. Overall, *Christopher Columbus: The Discovery* fails as an accurate portrayal of Columbus' first crossing and encounter with the peoples and locations in the New World. It is too contrived and looks cheap. The acting is sub-par and the character's actions and motivations are poorly developed. *New York Times* film critic Vincent Canby reviewed the film in August 1992 and had very little positive to say about the movie. He described the film as "a nonstop hoot," "sloppy," and "expensive," and he jibes Brando's portrayal of Torquemada "as if the face of the man in the moon had been perched on a great gray cassock, which serves as a sort of mobile plinth."

1492: Conquest of Paradise *(1992)*

Ridley Scott's film *1492: Conquest of Paradise* (1992) is the most ambitious of the films reviewed in this chapter. The film was released only a couple of months after *Christopher Columbus: The Discovery* (1992), both films celebrating the 500th anniversary of Columbus' first voyage. This film is perhaps more controversial than the other two films included in this chapter. The French actor Gérard Depardieu was cast to play Columbus, and his French accent throughout the film is

FIGURE 3.1 Gérard Depardieu as Columbus in *1492: Conquest of Paradise* (1992, Paramount Pictures).

odd in places, and completely unintelligible in others. He played Columbus as a conflicted visionary who tended toward megalomania at times. And, the film is more aspiring than the others in that it goes beyond Columbus' first voyage and deals with the subsequent colonization of the islands of the Caribbean.

The film begins with Columbus and his young son Fernando (who would become his father's biographer later); Columbus is teaching his son that the world it round by showing him an orange while also demonstrating that ships on the horizon disappear from view the farther they venture from land. Columbus is residing with Fernando's mother and his older son Diego near a Spanish monastery. Early in the film, the viewer is presented a graphic portrayal of an *auto-da-fé* (a public execution where victims are burned alive) being conducted by the Spanish Inquisition. No explanation is given for this scene. Soon thereafter, Columbus is granted an audience at the University of Salamanca. After explaining his methods and motives for a voyage, he is told by the authorities of the college that he will not be supported in his venture.

Sometime later, Columbus meets another sailor, Martín Alonso Pinzón, who for unknown reasons wants to help Columbus get an audience with the queen. Columbus has been waiting for just such an opportunity, and now with the fall of Granada, the last Muslim stronghold in Spain, this audience is close to becoming a reality. Unlike the previous two films, in *1492* the audience is not given the impression that the queen would need to sell her jewels. Instead, the cost of the voyage is estimated to be the same as two state banquets. In other words, the Spanish have little to lose by supporting Columbus, and everything to gain.

Columbus demands 10 percent of the wealth he would generate, titles of admiralty, viceroyalty, and nobility, and all this in perpetuity to him and his posterity. He is told he is too ambitious, whereupon he declares that if they can find someone else to take on the voyage he will become a monk. Isabella (played by Sigourney Weaver) relents and grants him permission and three ships owned by Martín Alonso Pinzón. He sets sail from Palos de la Frontera in August 1492. Ship-life is portrayed well and Columbus is also portrayed using an astrolabe to steer by. In reality, Columbus steered by a system of dead reckoning where maps and charts were used, in conjunction with measurement of speed which was accomplished by throwing a piece of wood over the side of the ship and then measuring how long it took to pass two fixed points on the ship's hull. This method of navigation is also portrayed on the film, and serves as the method whereby Pinzón and others realize Columbus is not keeping an accurate distance log of the journey. As Columbus' duplicity is discovered, the crew begins to grumble about the voyage but Columbus plays upon their sense of adventure and greed to prevent a mutiny and continue the crossing.

Columbus sights land first, which is in line with the later writings of his son and biographer Fernando. In a dramatic scene, he goes ashore in slow motion and falls to his knees on the wet sand. He names the island San Salvador and the Spaniards soon begin to explore the jungle. The encounters with Indians in this film are more realistic than those depicted in the previous two films discussed earlier. The Indians inspect the Spanish armor and beards. The two groups cannot communicate with each other. Columbus orders that the Indians be treated kindly, and then they realize that the Indians have some small trinkets made of gold.

At this point, one of the most glaring historical discrepancies takes place. The film makes no mention of the sinking of the *Santa María* on Christmas Eve. Instead, Columbus decides for no apparent reason to leave 39 men behind to build a fort. Then, the film shows all three ships departing for Spain. Columbus returns to Spain as a hero, and the film simultaneously depicts the death of Pinzón from some unnamed disease (Pinzón's death is commonly assumed to be from syphilis). At court, Columbus shows the nobility how to smoke tobacco. He also presents the Native Americans and their gold. Soon, Columbus is sent on a second voyage with 17 ships and more than 1500 men. After an hour and a half, this is where the film should have ended. But director Scott continues his narrative, and the second half of the film begins to break down.

Columbus selects his two brothers, Bartolomeo and Giacomo, to be governors of colonies in the New World—thus bypassing other Spaniards who were better qualified for such political positions—and by the end of 1493 they are back in the New World building a colony on the island of Hispaniola. Columbus clashes with the nobles who have journeyed with him, including the main antagonist in the second half of the film, Adrián de Moxica, played by Michael Wincott. Unfortunately, the Spaniards cannot find any trace of the 39 men who were left behind, except for some skeletal remains.

As they work to create the buildings and structures of the colony, the feud between Columbus and the nobility increases. Columbus insists that the nobility must work alongside the others, and incarcerates some nobles for abusing the Indians. While these episodes of infighting are taking place, the natives prepare for battle, and here Scott makes some strange decisions. When an Indian warrior charges Columbus, the sound of a roaring jaguar can be heard through the soundtrack. Then, when Columbus kills this Indian, the man squeals like a gutted boar. Scott seems to have been attempting the dramatic, but this dehumanization of the Indian warrior is odd and unnecessary.

Eventually, a Spanish noble named Francisco de Bobadilla arrives at the colony and takes control as the new governor of the Indies. He then sends Columbus back to Spain in chains. Columbus has his titles of governorship stripped from him, and he is humiliated and placed in prison. Columbus argues that if he was granted the opportunity to sail again, he would be able to discover the "Asian" mainland. He is told that it was discovered weeks ago by Amerigo Vespucci which is inaccurate; Columbus discovered the mainland in August 1498, while Vespucci didn't arrive in the Americas until 1499. Eventually Columbus is granted one last voyage by Queen Isabella. Here the film finally comes to an end as Columbus romantically gazes out to sea.

1492: Conquest of Paradise is broad and sweeping in its portrayal of Columbus. It is perhaps too ambitious in that it attempts to depict Columbus with all of his faults and his failures, whereas the previous two films discussed above end after the first voyage, thus escaping all of the controversy that clouded Columbus' later life. However, possibly Ridley Scott should be praised for his efforts, because history often forgets that Columbus sailed to the New World multiple times, and that while he was an excellent navigator, he was not a good governor or administrator in the Americas. So, while *1492* is more difficult to watch, it is arguably the most valuable and accurate of the three.

In October 1992, Roger Ebert reviewed *1492* and gave it more praise than condemnation. He praised Depardieu's interpretation of the conflicted Columbus, and he also extolled the portrayal of the scenery, the Native Americans, and the clashes present in the Spanish court at the time. His main criticism seems to be about the actual first voyage itself. "What disappoints me a little about Scott's version is that he seems to hurry past Columbus' actual voyage of discovery. There is intrigue in the Old World and adventure and violence in the New, but the crucial journey that links them seems reduced to its simplest terms: the three ships sail, the crews grow restless, there is mutiny in the air, Columbus quiets it, and then land is sighted." Ebert concludes by reminding viewers that "1492 is a satisfactory film. Depardieu lends it gravity, the supporting performances are convincing, the locations are realistic, and we are inspired to reflect that it did indeed take a certain nerve to sail off into nowhere just because an orange was round."

Notes

1 Christopher Columbus, "Letter of Columbus to various persons describing the results of his first voyage and written on the return journey," in *The Four Voyages*, pp. 115–122 (London: Penguin Books, 1969).
2 Ibid.
3 Ibid.

Further Reading

Bergreen, Laurence. *Columbus: The Four Voyages, 1492–1502*. New York: Penguin, 2012.
Columbus, Christopher, and J. M. Cohen. *The Four Voyages: Being His Own Log-Book, Letters and Dispatches with Connecting Narratives*. London: Penguin, 1992.
Keen, Benjamin. *The Life of the Admiral Christopher Columbus: By His Son Ferdinand*. New Brunswick, NJ: Rutgers University Press.
Morison, Samuel Eliot. *Admiral of the Ocean Sea*. Boston, MA: Little Brown, 1942.
Morison, Samuel Eliot. *Christopher Columbus Mariner*. New York: Signet, 1955.
Sale, Kirkpatrick. *The Conquest of Paradise*. New York: Knopf, 1990.
Sauer, Carl O. *The Early Spanish Main*. Berkeley, CA: University of California Press, 1966.
Symcox, Geoffrey and Blair Sullivan. *Christopher Columbus and the Enterprise of the Indies*. New York: Bedford/St. Martins, 2005.
Taviani, P.E. *Christopher Columbus*. London: Orbis Publishing Ltd., 1985.

4

THE SPANISH CONQUEST
OF LATIN AMERICA

I and my companions suffer from a disease of the heart which can be cured only
with gold.

Hernán Cortés

And when we saw all those cities and villages built in the water, and other great
towns on dry land, and that straight and level causeway leading to Mexico, we were
astounded . . . Indeed, some of our soldiers asked whether it was not all a dream . . .
It was all so wonderful that I do not know how to describe this first glimpse of things
never heard of, seen or dreamed of before.

Bernal Díaz

Introduction

Following Christopher Columbus' first voyage across the Atlantic Ocean, he
made three more journeys to the Western Hemisphere in his attempts to locate
Japan, China, and India. Right up to the point of his death in 1506, Columbus
continued to argue that he had sailed to Asia, a claim that other explorers in
the employ of Spain and Portugal were beginning to deny. By 1504, the same
year that Queen Isabella of Castile died, explorer, writer, and map maker Amerigo
Vespucci had made a couple of voyages to the New World for Portugal, and he
argued that it was not Asia at all, but in fact a new continent, a new world.
Based on the writings of Vespucci and others, a German cartographer named
Martin Waldseemüller labeled the new land mass "America" in 1507 on a new
world map.

The notion that a new world lay just over the western horizon, filled with strange new plants, animals, foods, peoples, and wealth, was exceptionally enticing to Spaniards and other Europeans for a variety of reasons. Wealthy and not-so-wealthy noblemen sought their fortune in the New World. Second sons who did not stand to inherit looked to the New World as a place of new beginnings and limited social hindrances. Clergymen saw the New World as a land ripe for proselytizing, a continent filled with vast groups of people in need of the gospel of Jesus Christ. But whatever their reasons, Spaniards, Portuguese, and other Europeans flocked to the Americas in ever-increasing numbers, searching for a new life in the New World. Of course, when the peoples and cultures of the Old World encountered and interacted with those of the New World, conflict was a frequent outcome. And, because of certain advantages discussed below, the European explorers and *conquistadores* managed to subdue countless numbers of Amerindians, while untold hundreds of thousands died from disease, warfare, and poverty.

The Conquest of Latin America

The conquest of Latin America took place throughout the sixteenth century and even into the seventeenth century in some locations such as the Maya highlands. The term "conquest" is habitually problematic because the overthrow of Latin America involved much more than just the military subjugation of the various Indian populations in the Americas. In addition to military strength, the conquest also involved an ecclesiastical transformation, as Indian religions were supplanted by Roman Catholicism; Indian social networks were disrupted by the Spanish Caste System; and Indian economic and agricultural practices were transformed by Spain's desires for silver and gold that they brought with them across the Atlantic Ocean. Nevertheless, all of these aspects of subjugation began in a few specific locations. The Spanish conquest of two major Amerindian civilizations of Latin America, the Aztecs of central Mexico, and the Inca of the Andes, set in motion Spain's eventual hegemony over most of the Western Hemisphere. Spain also conquered other Indian groups such as the Maya of Mexico and Guatemala, but the Maya conquest was not a simple matter of replacing a native centralized government with a Spanish one, and therefore the Maya conquest dragged on for more than 100 years.

The Conquest of the Aztecs

The Spanish military conquest of the Aztec Empire between 1519 and 1521 is in many ways the quintessential tale of how vastly outnumbered Spanish soldiers were able to topple a vast, powerful, politically centralized empire in a manner of months. This episode was also the legendary spark that spawned so many other attempts at domination throughout the Americas from Florida and California to Chile and the Amazon Basin.

The Spanish invasion of central Mexico is very much the story of Hernán Cortés and his skills as both a military tactician, and as a charismatic orator. But the story of Cortés begins years before his arrival on the eastern coast of central Mexico in 1519. Cortés sailed to the Caribbean islands in 1503 at the age of 18. As a second son, Cortés didn't have many prospects in Spain and so he was looking elsewhere for wealth and adventure. After his arrival in the New World, he soon began to make a living for himself in the colony of Santo Domingo, on the island of Hispaniola. Between 1511 and 1518, Cortés participated in a few conquest and discovery expeditions in the Caribbean, and by 1518 he was granted permission to lead an expedition to the Mexican mainland, west of the Caribbean islands. He was granted this opportunity by Cuban governor Diego Velasquez, a famous conquistador and explorer who had taken Cortés on some earlier voyages. But as Cortés prepared for this voyage to Mexico, Velasquez began to have second thoughts about Cortés' integrity, and tried to have him removed from command of the expedition. When Cortés learned of the impending change of plans, he committed an act of treason by gathering up his men and supplies, and sailing for Mexico before he could be stopped by the authorities.

Cortés first landed in Mexico on the Yucatan Peninsula, where he briefly interacted with groups of Maya Indians, and where he rescued a shipwrecked Spaniard named Gerónimo de Aguilar. Then, as Cortés continued down the west coast of Yucatan, he stopped again briefly in the modern area of Tabasco where he received a gift from the local Indians of several native women. One of these women, later referred to as Doña Marina, or more commonly as La Malinche, became very valuable to Cortés because she spoke both the local Maya dialect, and also Nahuatl, the language of the Aztec Empire, and thus was able to translate for Cortés in his interactions with the Mexican Indians.

Cortés and his men continued west and eventually landed on the Mexican gulf coast near the modern-day city of Veracruz in the spring of 1519. He is purported to have had between 500 and 600 soldiers with him, in addition to horses and artillery. Cortés attempted to legitimize his mutiny back in Cuba by founding a town council in Veracruz, and then accepting their charge to him that he lead an expedition to the interior of Mexico in search of wealth and conquest. After several months on the coast, Cortés began to march west toward the Aztec Empire that he had learned about through his interactions with local Indian tributaries who were forced to pay tribute to the Aztec emperor. As Cortés marched west, he encountered several different groups of Indians, most of whom were Aztec tributaries or allies. But a few groups, particularly the Tlaxcalans, were still enemies of the Aztecs and had resisted conquest for decades. Seeing the Spanish soldiers as potentially powerful allies, the Tlaxcalans sided with Cortés against their Aztec enemies and contributed Indian warriors to Cortés' expedition.

Early in November 1519, Cortés and his army were greeted by the Aztec emperor Moctezuma II and allowed to enter the Aztec capital city Tenochtitlán, an island-city in the middle of Lake Texcoco in central Mexico. Moctezuma was wary of Cortés because of his apparent association with Aztec enemies, and also because of several fearful premonitions that the superstitious Moctezuma had had over the previous months, but he nevertheless invited Cortés into the city. Motives for both men have been debated by historians repeatedly. Why would Emperor Moctezuma allow Cortés to enter the capital city if Cortés was a potential threat? Why would Cortés enter the capital city if it was, as he feared, a potential trap? Answers to these questions are enigmatic, but it seems that Cortés was sufficiently confident of his strength in terms of men, arms, and allies that he did not believe he could be defeated inside the city. For Moctezuma's part, many have speculated that he may have believed that Cortés was in fact or in part a reincarnation of the ancient central Mexican deity Quetzalcoatl, the feathered serpent god of the ancient civilizations of Mexico. Modern scholarship has cast greater light on Moctezuma's state of mind, superstitions, and beliefs surrounding the advent of the Spanish in Mexico, and it seems that he was somewhat paralyzed by indecision regarding how to interact with the Spaniards.

By the spring of 1520, Cortés and his men had been in Tenochtitlán for several months and they were becoming frustrated that they were not getting wealthy on Aztec gold. So, Cortés attempted to take control of the Aztec Empire by taking Emperor Moctezuma hostage and issuing orders through him. This attempt at controlling the Aztecs was interrupted when Cortés learned of a Spanish expedition from Cuba that arrived on the Mexican coast near Veracruz in April 1520 with orders to arrest Cortés for his mutiny and return him to Cuba to stand trial. Cortés took several hundred soldiers back to Veracruz to deal with this new challenge, and left one of his senior officers, Pedro de Alvarado, in charge of the remaining soldiers in the Aztec capital city. Ultimately, Cortés managed to not only avoid arrest, but also convinced the bulk of the soldiers who had been sent to arrest him to join with him instead. When he returned to Tenochtitlán in May 1520, he learned that Alvarado had recently ordered Spanish soldiers under his command to massacre a large group of Aztec nobles who had been participating in a religious festival.

Cortés was once again permitted to enter the city, but this time the tensions were high, and it seems that the Aztecs planned to ambush the Spanish all together inside the city where their artillery and gunpowder, weapons, and horses were less of an advantage to the *conquistadores*. When Cortés had the captive Emperor Moctezuma address the people of the city in an attempt to quell the tension, the Aztecs responded with hostility. What the Spanish did not understand was that when they had captured Moctezuma, his status as emperor of the mighty Aztec Empire had evaporated and he had been replaced as emperor. At this point in the narrative, Moctezuma died, but accounts of his death depend in large measure on the perspective of the source. The Spanish accounts claim that Moctezuma was hit in the head by stones that were hurled at him by his own people as he tried to address them, and that he died from his wounds not long after. Aztec accounts, on the other hand, argue that Cortés ordered Moctezuma garroted after realizing that he was of no worth to the Spanish in securing any further wealth, or in accomplishing a peaceful retreat from the island city.

Now the Spanish attempted an escape from the Aztec capital. On June 30, 1520, after dark had fallen, the Spanish made a run for it, attempting to flee across the main causeway that linked the Aztec city with the mainland on the lake shore. As the Spanish ran from the city under cover of darkness and rain, they were labored down with artillery, weapons, horses, and sacks of loot that they had taken while in the city. These items weighed then down in their flight, and when the Aztecs discovered their attempted retreat, they attacked the fleeing Spanish soldiers along the causeways. This night-time escape-turned-massacre became known as the *Noche Triste*, or sad night. Thousands of Indian warriors allied to the Spanish died that night securing the escape of the Spanish conquerors, and the Spanish themselves suffered losses estimated as high as 400 to 500 men. Most of the treasure and loot they attempted to carry out of the city ended up at the bottom of the lake.

The Spanish soldiers and their Tlaxcalan allies escaped to nearby Tlaxcala to measure their losses and plan their next moves. Between February and May 1521, Cortés and his soldiers built 13 small sailing vessels, or brigantines, that could be used on Lake Texcoco to lay siege to the Aztec city. These small vessels were then carried to the shores of the lake in pieces, constructed, and then sent toward the Aztec island-city; they were launched on April 28, 1521. The Spanish quickly captured the causeways and effectively prevented the city from obtaining food supplies from the mainland. The Spanish also cut off the water supply to the city by destroying the aqueducts that carried spring water to the island from the mainland.

From the start, the Aztecs and the Spanish fought several fierce skirmishes, but unbeknown to the Spanish, the Aztecs had suffered a massive outbreak of smallpox in the intervening months since the *Noche Triste*. The smallpox epidemic had been so devastating that thousands of Aztecs had died. Those who survived were often too weak to care for the sick, or for themselves, and they were unable to continue food production, leading to more deaths. The disease had also afflicted many of the leaders of the Aztec Empire; many high-ranking priests and political leaders had taken ill and died, including Moctezuma's replacement, the new emperor Cuitláhuac. As a result of the smallpox epidemic, the Aztecs were unable to resist the Spanish as forcefully as they might have under better conditions.

The final battles of the war were fought in the late summer of 1521, and much of the magnificent island city of Tenochtitlán was devastated in street-to-street fighting. Finally, after nearly three months of warfare and siege, Cuauhtémoc, the last Aztec emperor, surrendered and the Spanish took complete control of the Aztec capital. The conquest of the mighty Aztec Empire was over.

The Conquest of the Inca

The conquest of the Aztec Empire by the Spanish under the command of Hernán Cortés is the stuff of legends. Indeed, following Cortés' victory in central Mexico, thousands of Spanish would-be conquerors flocked to Mexico and other parts of Central and South America to attempt to duplicate his feat if they could. But perhaps no other episode of conquest in the New World compares to the conquest of the Inca Empire. When the Inca conquest is compared to the conquest of the Aztecs, several differences become apparent. The first major difference between the two events is the fact that the geographic size of the Inca Empire was enormous, stretching from Ecuador in the north, to Chile in the south, and from the Pacific coast on the west to the headwaters of the Amazon river and the Andes mountains in the east (a total of more than 750000 square miles, compared to less than 200000 square miles for the Aztec Empire). The terrain was also different; Peru's mountainous topography was much more difficult to navigate than the landscape in Mexico had been. In terms of manpower, the number of Spanish soldiers involved in the conquest of the Inca was dramatically smaller than the number involved in the conquest of Mexico. Finally, in terms of population, the Inca Empire, despite being vastly larger than the Aztec Empire in geographical terms, was sparser in demographics. The population of the Central Mexican Aztecs at the time of conquest is estimated to have been around 25 million. By contrast, the population of the Inca Empire is generally estimated to have held around 12 million people in the 1530s, at the time of contact with Europeans.

The foundation for the Spanish conquest of the Inca Empire began in 1513, when Spaniards in Central America first laid eyes on the Pacific Ocean from the Isthmus of Panama. From this point forward, the Spanish began to sail and explore the Pacific coast of South America, and soon heard tales of a wealthy and powerful Indian empire to the south in the mountains of Peru. And, just as the conquest of the Mexican Aztecs was in many ways the story of Cortés and Moctezuma and their decisions, so the conquest of the Inca focuses on a Spanish conquistador named Francisco Pizarro, and an Inca king named Atahualpa.

Francisco Pizarro was the illegitimate son of a Spanish military officer. He sailed to the New World in 1502 when he was in his mid-thirties and soon found his way to Central America. In 1513, Pizarro accompanied explorer Vasco Núñez de Balboa on the expedition that led the Spanish to the Pacific Ocean for the first time. By 1519, Pizarro held a political position in the ruling apparatus of the region, working as the mayor of Panama City. As early as 1522, stories began circulating in Panama of a wealthy empire to the south. Legends such as El Dorado and the Seven Cities of Gold spread rapidly, and were intensified by stories about Cortés and his legendary conquest of Mexico in 1521. The legend of El Dorado (or the Golden Man) was perpetuated in the late 1520s and early 1530s in many parts of Latin America. The legend stated that in an undiscovered Indian city, the king or emperor of the Indians was so wealthy that he covered himself completely in gold dust and shone with a brilliant golden light. Likewise, the Seven Cities of Gold were rumored to exist north of the Aztec/Mexican frontier, and the natives there were so fabulously wealthy that they built their homes and buildings out of gold. Rumors such as these only added to the gold fever that afflicted many Spaniards hoping to come to the New World and become marvelously rich.

In 1524, Pizarro decided to set out on an exploratory mission to South America to seek for lands of wealth and untold riches. However, Pizarro's first expedition was for the most part a complete failure. Fewer than 100 men sailed down the Pacific coast of Colombia, and endured hardships, starvation, and hostile Indians before they admitted defeat and turned back to Panama.

Pizarro's second expedition in 1526 was more successful as a whole, but still did not lead him to the famed wealth and glory he dreamed of. In the autumn of 1526, he again set sail from Panama, this time with nearly 200 men. They sailed along the Pacific coast of Colombia for several days and then divided their force into two groups. Pizarro's group explored the mainland along Colombia's southern coast, while a second group sailed further south under the leadership of Bartolomé Ruiz. And even though Pizarro himself did not make any dramatic discoveries on this second expedition, Ruiz did. Ruiz sailed south to a coastal village named Tumbez, south of modern Quito in Ecuador. There, he encountered Andean Indians who were actively trading in ceramic vessels and cloth, and even small quantities of gold and silver. Ruiz acquired some of these items and returned to report to Pizarro. Now reunited, Pizarro's entire group sailed south to Tumbez, and then continued further south along the Peruvian Pacific coast, where they came upon a small group of Incas for the first time. But, after a few unsuccessful skirmishes with the natives, the Spaniards decided to return to Panama for more supplies and men, with whom they would return and finish the conquest of the area.

However, when Pizarro requested permission to return to South America and the conquest of the Inca, the governor of Panama refused to allow Pizarro to undertake another expensive expedition, citing dangers and the costly nature of the voyages. Undeterred, Pizarro sailed to Spain where he petitioned King Charles I directly to allow him to continue his quest in the south. The monarch was eventually influenced by Pizarro's tales of wealth and glory, and granted him the official backing of the Crown. With his voyage to Spain successful and his permission to return to South America secured, Pizarro returned to Panama and began to prepare for his third journey to Peru. Pizarro's third and final voyage began in December 1531. He and his soldiers sailed down the Columbian and Ecuadorian coasts and eventually docked at Tumbez as they had done previously. Then, following Cortés' example from the conquest of Mexico, Pizarro founded a town called Piura to be used as a base of operations. Then, Pizarro began a march further into Peru.

What Pizarro did not realize when he entered the Inca Empire in the early months of 1532 was that the Inca had recently suffered two major setbacks. First of all, the Inca had only just endured a devastating smallpox epidemic that caused thousands of deaths, debilitating the Indians and disrupting their political and economic stability. In fact, the emperor of the Inca Empire, Huayna Capac Inca, had died of smallpox earlier in 1527. The second tragedy faced by the Inca was a civil war between two of Huayna Capac Inca's sons over the leadership of the empire in the wake of their father's untimely death. These two sons, Atahualpa and Huascar, both claimed legitimacy to rule, and both had armies in the field to secure territory, each from the other.

At one point, Huascar controlled the Inca capital city of Cuzco, and he even captured Atahualpa and briefly imprisoned him. But after Atahualpa managed to escape, he fled to the north, leaving the capital city of Cuzco in his brother's hands. By January 1531, Atahualpa's generals defeated his brother Huascar's army near Cuzco, and Huascar himself was captured and soon executed. At this point, Atahualpa became the new emperor of the Inca Empire. But, before marching south to occupy the city of Cuzco, Atahualpa and several thousand troops stopped at the northern city of Cajamarca. It was here in Cajamarca that Pizarro's Spanish *conquistadores* met Atahualpa and his army.

Atahualpa's advisors and military commanders were aware of Pizarro's presence in Peru, and they reported Pizarro's movements to Atahualpa in Cajamarca. But Atahualpa dismissed Pizarro and his soldiers as unimportant and trivial. After all, Atahualpa's scouts reported Pizarro's forces to number around 200 men and Atahualpa had with him near Cajamarca more than 70000 warriors. Pizarro soon sent envoys to request a meeting with Atahualpa. At first he refused, but then eventually he complied and agreed to meet Pizarro outside the city. The meeting took place on November 16, 1532. Atahualpa came in full regalia with an honor guard, but left most of his soldiers back in their camps. When the meeting began, Pizarro instructed an accompanying priest, Father Vincente de Valverde to approach Atahualpa and read a document to him called the *Requerimiento.*

The *Requerimiento* was an official Spanish edict, written in 1510, which was to be read to all Native American Indians when they first interacted with Spanish soldiers and priests. The document "required" the Indians to do several things, or suffer harsh consequences. Indian populations were obliged to: accept the Catholic Church and the pope as the leaders of the entire world; accept the monarchs of Spain as the stewards and governors of the New World; and accept Christianity as preached to them by the clergy. If Indian populations consented to these requirements, they would—according to the document—be left unmolested and free to go about their daily lives. If, however, they would not consent to the demands of the document, the Spanish were at liberty to declare war on the Indian populations, enslave them, confiscate their property, and "do you all the mischief and damage that we can." Furthermore, the document concluded that if, in the course of enforcing the *Requerimiento*, recalcitrant Indians died, their deaths were their own fault and not the responsibility of the Spanish soldiers, the monarchy, or the Catholic Church.

Father Valverde approached Atahualpa and read the document to him, and then purportedly held out a Holy Bible or breviary for the Inca ruler to accept. Atahualpa took the book, inspected it briefly, and then threw it to the ground. Father Valverde interpreted this action as a rejection of the conditions of the *Requerimiento*, and of Christianity in general, and retreated from the Inca ruler, whereupon Pizarro ordered his men to attack the emperor's retinue. When the fighting was over, around 2000 Inca warriors were dead and Atahualpa was captured. No Spaniards died in the fighting although some were wounded.

Next, Pizarro issued orders to the Inca leaders through Atahualpa, and was more successful than Cortés had been in using a puppet ruler to conquer a Native American empire. Pizarro ordered Atahualpa to have gold and silver brought to the Spanish, in addition to precious stones, cloth, and other luxury items. Atahualpa, on seeing the Spaniard's desires for precious metals, made Pizarro an offer. Atahualpa promised to fill the room in which he was standing (the room measured 12 feet wide, 17 feet long, and 6 feet high) completely with gold once, and with silver twice, in exchange for his freedom. Pizarro agreed and Atahualpa immediately sent soldiers out to bring in gold and silver from different areas of the Inca Empire. It took more than two months to accomplish the task, but when it was finished, the amount of gold that had filled the room weighed around 13000 pounds, and the amount of silver weighed nearly 26000 pounds. This was the single largest one-time looting accomplished by the Spanish in the New World. The silver and gold, in the form of precious works of art, was melted down into ingots for ease of transport and trade, and then distributed among Pizarro's men.

Atahualpa continued to live with Pizarro and the Spanish soldiers for nearly another year. Eventually, however, Pizarro and some of his advisors decided to have Atahualpa put to death, possibly because they feared an Inca insurrection aimed at rescuing the former emperor. In August 1533, Atahualpa was put on trial for various contrived crimes such as marrying his sister, practicing polygamy, and murdering his brother. At the end of the trial, he was convicted and sentenced to death by burning because of his non-Christian religious beliefs. Father Valverde later told Atahualpa that if he were to convert to Christianity, his death sentence would be carried out by strangulation instead of burning at the stake. Atahualpa agreed and was baptized, and then garroted immediately afterwards.

Following Atahualpa's death, Pizarro installed a new puppet leader, one of Atahualpa's younger half-brothers named Manco. Now, with Atahualpa dead and a new leader firmly under his control, Pizarro ordered his troops to march south to the Inca capital city of Cuzco. The city was captured in November 1533, and although Inca warriors attempted to recapture Cuzco and other Inca cities over the next few years, the Spanish remained firmly in control of the area. On January 5, 1535, Pizarro founded the city of Lima as the new capital city and center of Spanish government in South America. Pizarro built this city closer to the Pacific coast, which made it more accessible from the sea than Cuzco, which was higher in the Andes mountains. Eventually, Lima became one of the most important Spanish cities in the Americas, seat of the viceroyalty of Peru, and one of the last areas to break away from Spanish colonial control 300 years later.

Conclusions

The conquest and colonization of Latin America by Spain is one of the most important episodes in modern world history. This period in Latin America marks the contact between Europe and the Americas, and the interactions that eventually led to Spanish hegemonic control of much of the Western Hemisphere, bringing the Native American populations to suppression and defeat. Occasionally in ancient world history, powerful nation-states and empires subjugated their less sophisticated neighbors and ruled them for decades and even centuries. But never again, following the Spanish conquest of Latin America in the early 1500s, would a world power control so completely a region of the globe as vast as the Americas. Spanish *conquistadores*, with few prospects in Spain, suddenly became important and powerful in the New World, and a few of them became fabulously wealthy. And, for Spain itself, the prestige and power that resulted from the Spanish conquest of Latin America elevated Spain to a position of wealth and power in Europe unprecedented since the days of the Roman Empire. And while other European nations such as England and France would outmaneuver and get the better of the Spanish Empire over the course of the next two centuries, for a while, the Spanish Empire was the most powerful kingdom on earth.

Filmography

Even though the conquest of Mexico and Peru are among the most important, critical, and exciting episodes in early colonial Latin American history, no film-maker has tackled the task of putting these chronicles on film. Nevertheless, a few films exist that depict Spanish *conquistadores* in their desires to conquer and control large areas of Latin America. *Aguirre, the Wrath of God* (1972) and *The Other Conquest* (2000) are two that attempt to portray this period in the history of Latin America. *Aguirre* depicts acts of conquest from the Spanish perspective, while *The Other Conquest* tells the tale from the native Aztec point of view. And, even though nearly 30 years separate these films, they both have poignant moments that capture the emotion and sentiment of the conquest of Latin America from the viewpoint of both sides, as well as some of the initial results of these exchanges.

Aguirre, the Wrath of God *(1972)*

Werner Herzog's film *Aguirre, the Wrath of God* (1972) has attracted something of a cult following in the United States. It is a quirky, idiosyncratic piece of film that Herzog, with one of his most utilized actors, Klaus Kinski created in the early 1970s. Filmed in German, *Aguirre* tells the true tale of an expedition that took place in South America following Francisco Pizarro's conquest of the Inca in Peru. One of Pizarro's brothers, Gonzalo, led an expedition into the jungles of Peru near the headwaters of the Amazon River searching for the mythological city of El Dorado. The film opens with sweeping scenes of Spaniards trying to make their way through the densely forested mountains with their native guides. The difficulties faced by the Spaniards, such as carrying heavy equipment, cannons, and animals are all depicted. The conquered Indians who serve as guides and translators are apparently enslaved, and are treated poorly by the Spaniards throughout the film. Two women also go along with the travel party, both carried in palanquins, which further contributes to the burden of traveling through the harsh terrain. Finally, the Spanish are accompanied by a priest, Father Gaspar de Carvajal.

Under the leadership of Gonzalo Pizarro, Don Lope de Aguirre is the second in command of the expedition. After arguing with Aguirre about the best methods for traveling forward, Gonzalo decides to send an expeditionary force of a few men down the Marañón river for a week to look for gold and supplies. The remainder of the army is to wait for them to return. A captain named Pedro de Ursúa is selected to lead that party, along with Aguirre, and Father Carvajal who will accompany. Also in this expeditionary force are the two women mentioned earlier, who are revealed to be Ursúa's wife Flores and Aguirre's daughter Inez. This group starts down the river on rafts, but one of the rafts soon gets stranded on the opposite side of the river from the main group. After the men from the stranded raft are killed by unseen Indians, the voyage continues and the animosity between Aguirre and Ursúa escalates.

At this point, Ursúa decides to return to Gonzalo Pizarro's camp overland, considering the expedition a failure, and not worth the continued loss of life by hostile Indian groups. Aguirre argues against going back and tells the men in the advance party about Cortés and how he became wealthy when he disobeyed orders. Eventually an insurrection ensues between the followers of Ursúa and those of Aguirre, and in the contention, Ursúa is shot (not fatally) by one of Aguirre's followers. The company elects (somewhat under duress) a new leader named Fernando de Guzmán who is in effect Aguirre's puppet. In this exchange, an interesting conversation takes place between Ursúa's wife Flores and Father Carvajal. She asks the priest to do something to help her wounded husband who is now also incarcerated in a quickly constructed cell of sorts made out of wood. The priest replies that the Church has always been on the side of the strong, implying that he will continue to support the mission under the new leadership of Fernando de Guzmán and Don Lope de Aguirre. Here, Herzog seems to be implying that during the years of the Spanish conquest of Latin America, the Catholic Church, in its zeal for proselytizing and converting the native populations of the Americas, would follow strong leaders who could help them further their mission of conversion. Eventually, the new leader, Guzmán, reads a proclamation drawn up by Aguirre, declaring the group of explorers an independent kingdom, separated from Spain. Don Guzmán is then proclaimed emperor of El Dorado.

The advance company continues to drift down the river looking for food and wealth. They encounter Indians occasionally, and they even raid an abandoned Indian village for food and supplies. But Herzog leaves the appearance of the Indians to the imagination of the viewer; the Peruvian warriors who continually kill the Spanish one or two at a time are almost never seen on screen, but are instead implied, hiding behind a screen of green jungle forest and growth. Herzog may have done this in an attempt to signify that the conquest of the Indians in South America was extremely one-sided, and while the Indians did mount resistance—which in some cases was significant—they were ultimately unsuccessful in driving the Spanish from their lands.

Herzog tips his hat to the conquest of the Incas by Francisco Pizarro with a scene that imitates one of the acts from the actual capture of Atahualpa described above. Some Indians who appear of peaceful intentions are taken aboard one of the rafts and Father Carvajal hands one of them a Bible, saying that it is the word of God. When the Indian unceremoniously tosses the Bible aside, the Spaniards attack him for desecrating the Bible and the Holy Church. Then they continue to slowly float, now down the Orinoco river, but their supplies are dwindling and they are beginning to slowly starve.

Because of the difficulties they face floating on rafts down the river, they have only brought one horse, but because they can no longer feed the horse, they kick the horse off the raft, while one of the soldiers complains that it would have been better to eat the horse. Then, "Emperor" Guzmán is killed by unseen Indians while he sits in a makeshift latrine constructed on the back of his raft. Finally, the imprisoned Pedro de Ursúa is taken from the raft into the forest and hanged, while Indians continue to kill the party one or two at a time, and while infighting among the Spaniards threatens to drive them further apart.

Ultimately, only one raft is able to continue floating down the river, at an increasingly protracted and maddeningly sluggish pace. The Spaniards continue to slowly die from Indian arrows, hunger, thirst, and disease. Aguirre's daughter Inez, who has been accompanying the party on one of the rafts this entire time, is then killed when she inexplicably walks to the end of the raft and stares into the jungle, making it easy for the unseen Indians to shoot her. When this

FIGURE 4.1 Klaus Kinski as Aguirre in *Aguirre, the Wrath of God* (1972, Werner Herzog Filmproduktion).

happens, Aguirre goes completely insane. Herzog draws from the historical record at this point, giving Kinski dialog from Don Lope de Aguirre's historical statements. Aguirre declares that he will go on to conquer Mexico and Peru, and create a race of pure people by reproducing with his now dead daughter. In a final twisted salvo, Herzog ends the film with a lingering series of shots of Aguirre lurching around the raft, now swarming with monkeys, while all the other Spaniards lie about in the rictus of death. Aguirre proclaims to one of the monkeys that he is the wrath of God. Film critic Roger Ebert called this scene one of the most memorable he had ever seen.

Overall, *Aguirre, the Wrath of God* is an interesting if eccentric film that, despite a low budget and the problems of filming on location in Peru, does a fair job of portraying the attitudes and actions of some Spanish conquerors as they interact with Indians in South America, particularly the conquest of Peru, and other later expeditions to Chile and Colombia. Nevertheless, the film is peculiar in places and outright weird in others. Actor Klaus Kinski does a phenomenal job of portraying the increasing insanity and instability of Don Lope de Aguirre, and some commentators have observed that this could be, in part, because of the fact that Kinski himself was an eccentric who dealt with his own demons throughout his acting career.

In 1999, Roger Ebert reviewed this film and called it "one of the great haunting visions of the cinema." Of director Herzog, Ebert observed that "Of modern filmmakers, Werner Herzog is the most visionary and the most obsessed with great themes." At one point during the filming, Kinski went on a rampage and threatened to leave the film, whereupon Herzog actually aimed a gun at Kinski to force him to continue the film, and in order to achieve the mood of this film and to get the acting from Kinski that he envisioned. Ebert concludes, "What Herzog sees in the story, I think, is what he finds in many of his films: men haunted by a vision of great achievement, who commit the sin of pride by daring to reach for it, and are crushed by an implacable universe."

The Other Conquest *(2000)*

The Other Conquest (2000) begins in 1520 in Tenochtitlán—later Mexico City—with a summary of the Spanish conquest of the Aztecs. An Aztec artisan named Topiltzin (an Aztec word with connotations of divinity) wanders through the streets of the once beautiful Aztec capital city, observing the dead and the destruction that has come upon his people. One of the laudable elements of this film is the fact that it was filmed in both Spanish and Nahuatl, the language of the Aztec Empire.

In the film, Topiltzin creates a codex; a book made of bark paper that folds like an accordion. He paints characters and pictures on the pages of the book as a depiction of the history of his people. This is significant because codices such as this were in fact painted by Aztec and Maya artists and scribes in much the same way. Unfortunately, only a very few such codices survived the colonial period in Central Mexico, Guatemala, and the Yucatan. Topiltzin and a group of Aztecs hide the codex in a stone monument for safety. Then they begin to enact a sacrificial ceremony to appease their gods. The Spanish *conquistadores* enter the Aztec temple just as a woman's heart is ripped from her chest. These soldiers begin to kill some of the Aztecs who are performing the ceremony, but one of the Spaniards distressingly asks if they are to save the Aztecs by killing them. This statement brings up the conundrum the Spanish faced in dealing with the sacrificial practices of the Aztecs. The Spanish were placed in the situation of demanding that the Aztecs stop killing each other by sacrifice, and if the Aztecs did not comply, the Spanish would kill them in order to force them to submit.

Director Salvador Carrasco portrays the transformation of Aztec religion into Christianity with a specific scene wherein an Aztec statue is broken apart and replaced with an image of the Virgin Mary. The Aztecs who witness this scene seem to understand the importance of this form of religious conquest. Topiltzin is eventually taken to see Hernán Cortés. A woman named Isabel translates for them, much like La Malinche (mentioned above) translated for Cortés and Moctezuma. The Aztecs debate about whether or not they should adapt to

Spanish language and religion in order to survive, or if they should fight for their way of life even if it means their own deaths.

In due course, Topiltzin enters a monastery and begins training. He is given the Christian name Thomas. He is also given the ability to choose the Native world of the Aztecs or the Christian world of the conquerors. On the one hand, Thomas/Topiltzin becomes obsessed with the image of the Virgin Mary and what the statue is supposed to represent. On the other hand, he and Isabel try to figure out how to save their culture, customs, and religion despite Spanish efforts to stamp them out. Here we see a powerful representation of the religious blending that took place in Latin America after the Spanish conquest. This mixing of religious customs and traditions is in many cases called syncretism, and involves the adoption of new religious customs and beliefs, while at the same time holding onto doctrines and practices of the past. The result is a mixture that has elements of both religious traditions, but is not purely one or the other. Religious syncretism took place throughout Latin America following conquest, and in some locations in Latin America these combined beliefs continue to this day. It is with this process in mind that the film depicts Thomas/Topiltzin beginning to associate the Virgin Mary with the statue of the fertility goddess that the Spanish destroyed earlier in the film. To him, the Virgin and the fertility goddess become one and the same. This combination eventually makes Thomas ill because he is so fixated on the shared symbolism between the two. Eventually, he steals the statue of the Virgin Mary and with it in his arms, falls and dies as a symbol of both his native beliefs and the Christianity of the Spanish conquerors.

Overall, this piece of Mexican cinema is an interesting portrayal of not the actual events of the conquest themselves, but rather the effects of the Spanish conquest within Mexico. The film demonstrates the plight of the Aztecs following the destruction of their civilization and the difficult choices they were forced to make, choosing between their former culture and lifestyles, and the new religion and way of life that was forced upon them. The film is sad in a way because it represents the death of the Aztec culture. But the Aztecs themselves are not fully enfranchised into Spanish society, even after conversion to Christianity. Neither do they remain fully "Aztec," because their original culture has been changed by the new practices and religion of the Spanish, much in the same way that religions become syncretic as described above. Instead, the Aztecs who accept change seem to enter into a transcendental state of *nepantlism*, or the condition of being torn from their original way of life and forced into a new situation where they are accepted by neither the Spanish nor the Aztecs who refused to change. In effect, they become something different and new that is a composite of the two cultures, representing portions of both, but effectively becoming a new culture, religion, race, and way of life. Director Carrasco has used his film to continue the debate over the pros and cons of the Spanish conquest of the Aztecs. He asks the important questions and has his actors play out scenes designed to place these challenges before his audience, forcing the viewer to choose a side.

Further Reading

Clendinnen, Inga. *Ambivalent Conquests*. Cambridge: Cambridge University Press, 1987.
de Diaz Canseco, María Rostworowski. *History of the Inca Realm*. Cambridge: Cambridge University Press, 1999.
De Landa, Diego. *Yucatan Before and After the Conquest*. Dover: Courier Corporation, 1978.
Díaz, Bernal. *The Conquest of New Spain*. London: Penguin Classics, 1963.
Hassig, Ross. *Mexico and the Spanish Conquest*. London: Longman, 1994.
Leon-Portilla, *The Broken Spears; The Aztec Account of the Conquest of Mexico*. Boston, MA: Beacon Press, 1990.
Moseley, Michael E. *The Incas and Their Ancestors*. London: Thames & Hudson, 2001.

5

IMPERIALISM AND COLONIALISM

O how small a portion of the earth will hold us when we are dead, who ambitiously
seek after the whole world while we are living.

King Philip II of Spain

Introduction

Following the military conquest of regions of Latin America, the imperial powers of Spain and Portugal faced a new dilemma that had to do with governing
their new overseas empires. Spain's new empire encompassed much of the territory from southern North America, all the way to the southernmost tip of
South America. For Portugal, their Western Hemisphere empire was comprised
of the massive colony of Brazil, which was smaller in size that Spain's American
empire, but was itself an enormous colony full of natural resources and native
inhabitants.

One of the most important questions regarding the colonial years of Latin
American history (1492–1825) focuses on how the Iberian countries of Spain
and Portugal maintained control over their Latin American colonies for more
than 300 years. When one considers the incredible obstacles, the logistics, and
the manpower involved in colonial Latin American history, it is easy to recognize
the unique and fascinating aspects of this episode in early modern world history.
For starters, the Amerindian populations in Latin America were vastly larger that
the number of Spanish and Portuguese settlers and soldiers who relocated to the
New World. Scholars estimate that in the year 1500, the native population of
Latin America would have been somewhat fewer than 50 million Indians. When
compared to the number of Spanish and Portuguese in the hemisphere at the

same time—likely fewer than 600000—the vast disparity of population is easy to see. And even though countless millions of Native American Indians died throughout the first half of the sixteenth century because of disease, warfare, and other complications, they still overwhelmingly outnumbered the European explorers and settlers.

Further complicating Spain and Portugal's ability to hold on to their colonies was the logistical reality that the distance from the Iberian countries to their Latin American colonies was, depending on the destination, between 3000 and 4000 miles. Columbus made the journey from the Canary Islands to the Bahamas in 36 days in 1492 (September 6–October 12), but voyages to Mexico, Peru, and other colonies in the New World took much longer. The Portuguese captain Pedro Cabral who first sailed to Brazil from Portugal made the voyage in 44 days (March 9–April 22). However, the physical distance between the Old and New Worlds was not the only difficulty in travel between the two. Storms, pirates and privateers, mutiny, lack of supplies, and a host of other problems hindered Iberian sailors from frequent, rapid transit across the Atlantic Ocean.

Dividing the World

Because both Spain and Portugal occupied territory in the Americas, the threat of hostile encounters along poorly defined borders became more of a reality, and the business of maintaining the colonies depended on settling or eliminating these disputes. Furthermore, now that Spain was successfully sailing across the Atlantic Ocean, the Portuguese feared that their own Asian trade routes could be compromised if Spanish ships began sailing east as well. In 1493, the potential for conflict between Spain and Portugal was taken up by the pope in Rome. In that year, Pope Alexander VI, originally from Spain, proclaimed a line of demarcation which effectively divided the Atlantic Ocean and Western Hemisphere between these two countries. An imaginary line was drawn from pole to pole, 100 leagues west of the Cape Verde Islands in the Atlantic. Portugal was granted rights of trade and transit east of the line, and Spain was granted the same rights on the west of the line. And, in addition to the granting of trade and commercial rights in their respective hemispheres, Spain and Portugal were also charged by the pope with the evangelization of the native inhabitants of all the lands they encountered and traded with.

Almost immediately, Portugal protested the placement of the papal line and suggested that the line be moved 370 leagues west instead of 100 leagues. Scholars have argued about this specific request—which was eventually granted by the pope in 1494, and was called the Treaty of Tordesillas. Why would Portugal make such a specific request in terms of the number of leagues west of Cape Verde? Some have posited that even though Portugal did not officially announce the discovery of Brazil until 1500, they likely knew that it was there, even as early as 1493, and wanted to keep as much of the territory on their side of the line as possible. Finally, in 1529, the placement of the line on the other side of the globe in the Pacific Ocean was finalized in the Treaty of Zaragoza which divided Spanish and Portuguese holdings in the Eastern Hemisphere as well. The line was set at 300 leagues east of the Moluccas, which put the Philippine Islands firmly in Spanish control, and left China and India to the Portuguese.

The Colonial Enterprise

Between the early 1500s and 1825, Spain and Portugal administered their colonies in the New World through a series of institutions that were designed to maintain Iberia's hegemony over the colonies, despite all of the logistical liabilities mentioned above. Throughout this 300-year period, colonialism evolved into an effective, if cumbersome, administrative mechanism that kept the colonies firmly under Iberian control while at the same time allowing for the export of raw materials and bullion back to the mother countries. Colonialism was the product of a new social order that placed Native Americans and those of mixed race at the bottom of the social hierarchy, and kept the minority Spanish and Portuguese settlers at the top. Of course the military aspects of conquest had occurred first and, by the mid-1500s, occurred less frequently. But the administration of the colonies became the major focus for the Iberians. Four principal institutions became centerpieces of royal policy in the New World: economics, politics, religion, and race.

Economic Colonialism

The economic control of the New World was perhaps the most significant and important element in long-term Spanish and Portuguese control. Institutions that forced native Indians to produce natural resources evolved into forced labor mechanisms that focused on agricultural and mineral wealth for the colonists. *Encomienda* and *repartimiento* were two such institutions. *Encomienda* was a system of Indian labor in which a Spanish soldier or settler was granted a specific plot of territory, including all the agricultural and mineral products found thereon, and also access to all the native Indians who lived on this land grant. This Spanish settler could then demand that the Indians who lived on his land work for him, either in production of agricultural commodities such as corn, tobacco, or potatoes, ranching products such as cattle and chickens, or in mining for the precious ore that was located in several areas of the New World. Indians who labored in agricultural and ranching activities were given quotas to fill and had to labor to meet these demands without compensation in a monetary form. Furthermore, the Indians were kept in perpetual debt to the landowners so that they could not simply pick up and leave the area.

Repartimiento, by contrast, was a system of forced labor that did not involve a specific territory of land where Indians were required to remain. Under *repartimiento*—sometimes also referred to as *mita* labor—Indians were used as laborers in a variety of projects throughout the Spanish and Portuguese Empires such as the construction of buildings, roads, bridges, tending livestock, acting as porters who carried goods and even people from place to place, and as household servants. And, whereas under *encomienda*, Indians were only used for mining if precious metals were found on that particular tract of land, under *repartimiento*, Indians could be forced to labor in mines found anywhere in the region.

Mining was one of the most important economic activities in the New World. Spanish and Portuguese officials used mining as a way to gain monetary wealth, pay taxes to the Crown, and also control Indian populations. The richest mining areas in the New World were found in Mexico, Bolivia, and Brazil. These areas were mined predominantly for silver in rich veins such as those in Zacatecas, Mexico and Potosí, Bolivia. Gold was also mined in Brazil and Colombia and a handful of other locations, but gold was never as prevalent as silver in the New World economic enterprises of the Iberian empires. For Spain and Portugal, the concept of mercantilism was somewhat modified from classical mercantilism as practiced by the British in their North American colonies. Under classical mercantilism, the role of the colony was to enrich the mother country by providing natural resources and raw materials that were shipped to the mother country, manufactured into finished products, and then sold back to the colony and to other countries as well. By contrast, Spanish and Portuguese mercantilism was somewhat underdeveloped in its conception and implementation. First of all, instead of natural resources, the Iberian colonies produced predominantly bullion to ship back to Spain and Portugal across the Atlantic Ocean. Second, because bullion required very little manufacture, the Iberian mother countries developed very little industry for the production of finished products and consumables. Instead, Spain and Portugal used the specie they imported from the Americas to purchase finished products from the English, the Dutch, and other European producers.

The results were devastating. Spain spent around 60 percent of its annual revenue on military expenditures, and less than 5 percent on public works projects and improvements. Even more shocking is the fact that around 15 percent was spent on the royal house itself, to maintain the lifestyle of the monarchs and their families. Inflation became a serious problem, and Spain and Portugal had very little to show for the money they generated. The long-term results were very negative. While English mercantilism produced manufacturing and industry for the mother country, which eventually led to the British Industrial Revolution, the predominant industry in Spain remained wine and olive oil production from vineyards, saffron, and sheep ranching. But even though Iberian economic development lagged behind other areas of Europe, these economic practices were only one factor that enabled them to maintain control of their Latin American colonies for more than 300 years.

Political Colonialism

In terms of political control, the Iberian kingdoms used a system of political manipulation and overlapping jurisdictions to maintain political power in their Latin American colonies. Because the monarchs resided in Spain and Portugal, it was not possible for them to oversee all of the political enterprises of the colonies directly. In fact, no Spanish monarch ever even visited one of the Latin American colonies, and only one Portuguese monarch did so, but not until the 1800s. Instead, the monarchs used the office of viceroy to control the daily political functions of their empires in the New World. Four separate viceroyalties were established in the Spanish colonies (Mexico, Peru, Argentina, and Colombia) while the Portuguese used a single viceroyalty for the massive colony of Brazil. The viceroys made decisions of major importance and acted, for all intents and purposes, as the king's eyes and ears in the colonies. Communication between viceroys and the king were slow and inefficient, but this was the only system that the Iberian kingdoms could use to maintain political control in their colonies.

Under the jurisdiction of the viceroys, a complicated apparatus of governors, lawyers, officials, mayors, and city council members existed to run the daily machinery of the empire and to maintain political power in the colonies. Politically, the Native American Indians had very little control and were labeled as inferior participants in society; as a result they had very few political rights.

Venality, or the sale of public office, occurred rather frequently in the New World colonies. And while the government apparatus discussed above was not terribly efficient or even competent at times, venality made it much worse. One of the ways the Spanish Crown tried to generate increased revenue for the royal treasury back home was through the sale of public political offices in the New World. As a revenue-maker, venality worked quite well. On the other hand, the individuals who ended up with positions of political power such as the governors, mayors, legal councilors, and even the viceroys, were not necessarily qualified for these positions based on their personal credentials. Instead, the bureaucratic machinery of some locations in the New World was staffed by those who had the money to pay for the job, whether they had a mind for politics or not. Later, during the mid-1700s, the practice of venality was discontinued because King Charles III correctly realized that the sale of public office not only placed incompetent individuals in positions of political power, but also that these individuals were not above corruption and ended up costing the Crown more in the long run than they generated in the short term.

Religious Colonialism

Religion was one of the driving forces behind Spanish exploration and colonization in the New World. Religion also played a role in the Portuguese Empire, but to a lesser degree than in Spain's holdings. In terms of colonialism, religion was one of Spain's primary tools for justifying their position in the western hemisphere, in converting Indians to Catholicism, and in maintaining a tight grip on the colonies. Indeed, Spanish soldiers arrived in the New World to conquer Indian civilizations and subdue them for the Spanish Crown. But Spanish priests came to conquer Indian souls and save them for the kingdom of God.

The ecclesiastical army that arrived in the Spanish territories in the Americas consisted of both secular and regular clergy. The secular clergy existed for the benefit of the Spanish and Portuguese settlers who came from their homes across the Atlantic Ocean and settled in the Latin American colonies. These were the priests, bishops, archbishops, and other ecclesiastical personnel who resided in Spanish cities and administered to the urban populations of the empire. On the other hand, the regular clergy consisted of mendicant orders such as the Dominicans, Franciscans, Jesuits, and others. These regular clergymen dedicated their time and resources to directly engage with the Indian communities in the New World. Regular clergymen learned Indian languages and dialects, lived in or near Indian communities, and oversaw the proselytizing of Indian tribes and villages.

One practice that became synonymous with the evangelism of the regular clergy was the construction of missions. Because the regular clergy worked closely with Native American populations in rural settings, it was necessary to create central meeting locations where church services could be held; where Indians could reside in larger numbers, and where education could take place. Missions were just such locations. More than simply church buildings, missions were community centers where Indian groups congregated (and even resided) to hear the word of God and to receive a Spanish-centered education. The ultimate goal of the missions, and the priests who oversaw them, was the transformation of Native American Indians into productive Spanish citizens. So, religious indoctrination, combined with education in European styles of dress and grooming, along with instruction in the Spanish language, all played a role in the success of the mission. And, because the missions were far away from the urban centers of the New World, the potential for conflict between Indians and Spaniards, and between regular and secular clergy, was somewhat diminished.

One of the products of religious evangelization among the Indians of Latin America was the occurrence of religious syncretism (also discussed briefly in Chapter 4). Syncretism was the blending of religious beliefs. The Spanish priests hoped that they would be able to replace Indian beliefs with the doctrines of the Catholic Church. But Indian religious traditions that had been in place for thousands of years were not so easily supplanted by the new teachings about Jesus Christ. So, instead of replacing Indian traditions, polytheism, and practices, Christianity frequently blended with Indian beliefs creating new, syncretic ideas that were neither purely Indian, nor wholly Christian.

Disease and hostility frequently plagued the Indian populations in the missions. Indians who had little or no resistance to European diseases were often exposed to these diseases in the close quarters of the missions. And, hostilities broke out when Indian groups that had been traditional enemies for centuries were placed in close proximity inside the mission territories. But for the most part, the priests who ran the missions attempted to overcome these obstacles and instruct the Indians in the paths of productive Spanish citizenry.

Racial Colonialism

One final element of Iberian colonialism in the New World was the reality of racial designation and ethnic identity. This was very much a cultural conquest where European standards of food, clothing, language, art, music, literature, and skin color all supplanted Indian cultural standards and skin color. Europeans in general viewed this aspect of colonialism as fair-skinned Europeans appropriately dominating the darker-skinned Indians and their mixed-race offspring, yet caring for and instructing them in a paternalistic way. To this end the Spanish and Portuguese created a caste system with levels and social hierarchy determined by skin pigmentation. *Limpieza de sangre*, or blood purity was the defining characteristic of one's social level, and rights and privileges in society depended on this blood purity, which was outwardly demonstrated by the color of one's skin.

The Spanish caste system, or *castas* as it was called, was far more complex than other examples of racial/social designation (such as, for example, the caste system in India, which contains four general levels). Some scholars have determined that there were dozens and dozens of levels in the Spanish caste system, all based on parentage and skin color. For example, the child of a Spanish father and Spanish mother was known as a Spaniard. But the child of a Spanish parent and an Indian parent was a *Mestizo*. A child of a Spanish parent and an African parent was called a *Mulatto*. Other combinations were also designated. Spanish and Mestizo produced a *Castizo*; Spanish and Mulatto produced a *Morisco*; Indian and Mestizo produced a *Coyote*; Indian and African produced a *Lobo*; and there were many others. Some of the terms were quite degrading – for example the two terms above, Coyote and Lobo (wolf). Other terms further down the list were even more disparaging such as *Torna Atras* (Backwards); *Tente en el Aire* (Up in the Air); and *Allí te Estás* (There You Are).

Conclusions

These kinds of tautological reasons—economic, political, religious, and racial—served as a catalyst for endemic Iberian control of Latin American society, and reduced Indians, Africans, and mixed-race peoples to second-class citizens or worse. The end of colonialism in Latin America in the 1820s resulted in the end of some of these institutions as well. But, in many ways, the vestiges of these colonial practices are still felt in Latin America today. Some examples could include the way religions are viewed and practiced, the economic underdevelopment of many areas of Latin America, and the continued use of the term "Mestizo" to self-identify racial heritage in the populations of many modern Latin American countries.

Filmography

There exists a dearth of good historical drama on the colonial period in Latin American history. Hopefully in the future more attention will be paid to creating films about Latin America's colonial period. Films about mining in Mexico and Bolivia, the sugarcane mills and plantations in the Caribbean and Brazil, and the role of religion in society throughout Latin America would all be welcome subjects in the corpus of film on Latin Americas colonial history. One of the films that captures the mood and spectacle of colonial Latin America is *The Mission*. This film outlines the colonial strategies employed by the Spanish and Portuguese during the 1700s, and also depicts what happens to the Native Indians who are caught in the middle of power-hungry men and their religious/political infighting.

The Mission *(1986)*

Roland Joffé's film *The Mission* (1986), written by Robert Bolt (*Lawrence of Arabia* and *Doctor Zhivago*) is a fantastic piece of historical drama set against the backdrop of Jesuit priests fighting for the survival of mission communities in Guaraní territory in Brazil and Paraguay in the 1700s. The film is a brilliant vehicle for transmitting visual drama that encompasses all of the historical elements of colonial society in Spanish and Portuguese South America. The colonial period, as mentioned above, was really a combination of several factors including the influence of the Church, local and international economics, colonial and national politics, and racial discrimination, all of which were present throughout Latin America prior to the 1800s. *The Mission* does a laudable job of portraying all of these aspects and bringing them seamlessly to the screen.

With regard to the Church, *The Mission* depicts several aspects of religious life in colonial society. Native Indians are depicted in church mission buildings learning to sing and play musical instruments. They even learn the skills necessary to make instruments such as violins and flutes. Priests of mendicant orders such as the Jesuits travel through inhospitable terrain to teach, convert, and live among Indian groups in the South American jungles. These Jesuits become protectors of the Indians, defending them from the ravages of slavery, which was practiced in both Spanish and Portuguese territories, although in the former it was considered illegal by the 1700s.

During the course of the film, a former mercenary and slave trader named Rodrigo Mendoza (played by Robert De Niro) becomes a Jesuit priest and renounces his former violent life. He eventually lives in the mission with the

FIGURE 5.1 Robert De Niro as Mendoza in *The Mission* (1986, Warner Bros).

Guaraní Indians and helps them learn the lessons of Christianity while he also learns and comes to love their culture and society. When political forces threaten to close the missions because of the proposed redrawing of the line demarcating the Spanish and Portuguese territories that existed all the way back to the Treaty of Tordesillas of 1494, Mendoza and the other Jesuits become involved in the political and religious struggle to maintain control of the Indian lands, and to prevent them from being enslaved by Portuguese slave traders.

Throughout the film, it is repeatedly demonstrated that while the political courts of Spain and Portugal are not particularly religious in nature, they often bow to the wishes of the Church for the benefit of both. The monarchs of Spain and Portugal are described as Christian kings, and thus they are held under certain obligations to endorse Christian laws and ordinances throughout their empires. Nevertheless, even though the Church had much political power in the seventeenth and eighteenth centuries in Latin America, ultimately world politics and economic gain succeeded in trumping the will of the Church.

The Mission is also replete with examples of the economics of empire. Slave hunters move through the jungles hunting the Guaraní Indians to sell as slaves. Slavery of Native Indians was illegal in the Spanish Empire, but slaves were still sold as contraband property. The Portuguese on the other hand permitted Indian slavery and, as the film progresses, the mission territories in question were to be transferred from Spanish control to Portuguese. This endangers the lives of the Guaraní because they will then be fair game for Portuguese slave hunters.

The film depicts plantations that function alongside mission territories. These plantations grow produce and care for animals. The Indians in the missions also produce handcrafted items such as musical instruments and cloth. The proceeds are used to supplement the coffers of the Church, and are then reinvested in the missions, where they can use the money to expand their holdings and continue their way of life.

The Mission is full of political discussions and implications. At the beginning of the film, Mendoza kills his brother in a duel because they both desire the same woman, Carlotta. Because it was a duel sparked by jealousy and infidelity, Mendoza is not prosecuted for any crime in the killing of his brother. This is an interesting development in the film because usually in colonial Spanish society, women who were sexually active outside of marriage were looked down upon and even persecuted for tarnishing the honor of their family. But in *The Mission*, Carlotta was pursued by both men, and was apparently also sexually active with both as well.

In terms of political borders, the film outlines the territorial expansion desired by the Portuguese in Brazil, while at the same time depicting the Spanish Crown's desire to ensure that Portuguese territorial enlargement will not happen at Spain's expense. However, both Crowns agree that the Jesuits are too powerful in South America and need to be subdued. In fact, during the course of the film, the Jesuits are effectively banned from the Portuguese Empire and are soon to be banned from the Spanish Empire as well, a historical fact that took place between 1759 in Portugal's holdings, and in 1767 in Spain's territories.

An interesting blending of politics and religion is depicted in the person of Cardinal Altamirano, the Church's representative who is sent to make the final decision about the mission territories. On one hand, he represents the Church, and at one point in the film he states that he himself was once a Jesuit. But, he also represents the Crown of Spain in this official inquiry and thus Altamirano is a combination of both state and Church authority.

Finally, the film references the Treaty of Madrid of 1750, which redrew the boundaries between Portuguese Brazil and Spanish South America. This treaty effectively abrogated the Treaty of Tordesillas that originally granted Portugal the right to administer the Brazilian colony, but limited the Portuguese to a narrow strip of territory on the Atlantic coastline of the South American continent.

Race and ethnicity are prominent themes in *The Mission*. The native Guaraní are portrayed throughout the entire film, along with the effects of slavery on Indian populations. Another social construct portrayed in the film is the role of the Mestizo. Mestizos, or individuals who had a Spanish parent and an Indian parent, are depicted throughout the film, including a Mestizo priest who oversees the indoctrination of the Indians at one of the Spanish missions. Finally, the film develops the differences between Peninsular Spaniards (those born in Spain) and Creole Spaniards (individuals with two Spanish parents who were born in

Latin America). Mendoza, for example, represents the Creole Spaniard social construct, whereas Cardinal Altamirano holds a higher level in society because of his Iberian birth.

Socially, the film draws attention to the differences between Spanish cities and the settlements on the outskirts of civilization. Spanish urban populations are portrayed as sophisticated groups of individuals, who inhabit permanent buildings, carry out transactions on streets, and who generally uphold Spanish traditions. The film also shows city life as a medium for festivals and celebrations. At one point, the film depicts a bull fight, and we also see carnival-type celebrations where people parade in the streets carrying idols and saints in religious processions. Spaniards and Mestizos alike participate in these activities.

Finally, the role of the Spanish and Portuguese military, an important element of Latin American colonial society, is portrayed well in the film. The conquest of the massive Indian empires in the 1500s represented the ability of the military to take control of huge swaths of territory and to subjugate the Indian populations. But, following the military conquest of Latin America, the Iberian military forces continued to play a role, keeping the peace and putting down insurrections for the general good of colonial society. In *The Mission*, after all the politicking is completed and the fate of the missions is decided, the military comes into the equation to settle the score once and for all. Because the Jesuits refuse to leave the missions and abandon their Indian charges, the Portuguese military prepares to drive the Jesuits from the missions, or kill them in the process. And even though some of the Jesuits, including Mendoza, attempt to defend the missions with weapons, they are no match for the organized army, which has firearms, cannons, and perhaps most importantly, free (i.e., non-mission) Indian allies who help to slaughter the mission Indians and priests who lead them.

The Mission stands alone as one of the best films depicting life in colonial Latin America. All of the elements and institutions of colonialism are illustrated in the film, and the relationships between these organizations are fully developed. And, while it is regrettable that more films portraying this historical period have not been produced, this film does a fantastic job of representing the lives of the individuals who lived and worked in this important period of Latin American history. However, some critics downplayed the importance of the film. In the *New York Times* in 1986, Vincent Canby observed: "The Indians, about whom the film seems to care so much, are condescended to as mostly smiling, trusting undifferentiated aspects of Eden." Roger Ebert, also writing in 1986, noted, "There isn't a moment in *The Mission* that is not watchable, but the moments don't add up to a coherent narrative. At the end, we can sort of piece things together, but the movie has never really made us care." Later in his review, Ebert concluded by suggesting that *The Mission* "hardly seems to have a center and feels like a massive, expensive film production that, once set in motion, kept going under its own momentum even though nobody involved had a clear idea of its final direction" (http://rogerebert.com).

Further Reading

Adelman, Jeremy. *Colonial Legacies: The Problem of Persistence in Latin American History.* New York and London: Routledge, 2012.

Boyer, Richard. *Colonial Lives,* Oxford: Oxford University Press, 1999.

Fisher, Andrew B., and Matthew D. O'Hara. *Imperial Subjects: Race and Identity in Colonial Latin America.* Durham, NC: Duke University Press, 2009.

Galeano, Eduardo. *Open Veins of Latin America.* New York: Monthly Review Press, 1997.

Restall, Matthew. *Seven Myths of the Spanish Conquest.* Oxford: Oxford University Press, 2004.

Restall, Matthew. *Latin America in Colonial Times.* Cambridge: Cambridge University Press, 2011.

6

THE AFRICAN ATLANTIC SLAVE TRADE IN LATIN AMERICA

Hatred, slavery's inevitable aftermath.

José Martí, Cuban revolutionary

African Slavery in the New World

Just a few years after Christopher Columbus sailed to the New World in 1492, Queen Isabella of Spain issued an interesting decree. She said that she did not "give permission to come [to Latin America] Moors, nor Jews, nor heretics, nor persons newly converted to our faith, except for Negro slaves." In this manner, in the early 1500s both Spain and Portugal began to lay the foundations for the greatest forced migration in human history, the African Atlantic Slave Trade. Slavery soon became the most important economic venture in the history of the hemisphere. Historically, the first ships carrying African slaves to the Western Hemisphere were Spanish vessels, arriving between 1502 and 1518 in ports on Caribbean islands such as Cuba, Jamaica, and Hispaniola. Slavery continued legally in the Spanish colonies until 1886, and until 1888 in Portuguese Brazil.

Over the more than 370 years that the slave trade operated on the coastlines of the Atlantic Ocean, it is estimated that roughly 11 million Africans died as a result of slavery, and a staggering three million died en route on the ships, or in Africa before they could be transported to the Americas. The voyage across the Atlantic was treacherous to say the least. Africans were crammed into ships to tightly that they often suffered wounds, bruises, abscesses, dysentery, and death. Many were locked in the holds in the bottom of ships and shackled together with large chains. On the worst voyages, it is estimated that one out of every five slaves died on the ships. Once in the New World, African slaves had to undergo a period of adjustment to the new food, climate, culture, and the intensive labor that was expected of them. All of these rigors meant that slaves constantly died and had to be replaced by more Africans from across the ocean.

Why did the Europeans not use Native American Indians as a labor force? Why go to all the logistical trouble and expense of bringing Africans across the Atlantic Ocean? One answer to these questions was the fact that the Native Americans were familiar with the terrain and landscape of the regions of the New World where they lived, and when they were enslaved, they found it easier to run away, and resorted to flight more often than Africans could or did. Another reason was the fact that the Indian populations were unable to deal with the rigorous labor that was required, and so they often died from exhaustion and other work-related issues. Finally, Native Americans were already dying in the tens of thousands because of exposure to European diseases, and this made it impossible to maintain them as slaves, especially when the slave force was constantly in need of replenishment.

On the other hand, Africans had interacted with Europeans for centuries, and had developed immunities to European diseases, so they did not suffer the same disease-based mortality rates as the Indians. However, they did suffer and die from other causes. Africans were considered property, and their owners had unlimited authority over them. The act of killing a slave who ran away or broke rules was an authority any slave-owner could use with impunity. However, this did not happen as often as other methods of punishment because slaves were valuable property and killing them would mean the owner could no longer use the slave to recoup the price paid for the slave in the first place. Plus, slaves died of other causes in such high numbers that murdering them was not seen as an effective method of control. Instead, slave-owners used corporal punishment in ways that punished misbehavior and disobedience, but simultaneously in ways that did not cause labor shortages or limit a slave's ability to work. The goal in punishment was to inflict pain, and to create an example to others, but not diminish the recalcitrant slave's productivity. Unruly slaves were sometimes branded, beaten, or whipped. In other instances, ears and noses were sliced, or tongues removed, all of which inflicted suffering while allowing the slave's productivity to continue.

Slaves in Latin America worked in a variety of enterprises and in many different locations. Slaves were transported to Brazil in huge numbers. Other Africans were taken to northern South America, Central America, and the Caribbean Islands. They worked on plantations that produced predominantly cash crops such as coffee, tobacco, cotton, cacao, gold and silver, and especially sugarcane. They also occasionally worked on garden plots, cultivating produce and other food items. Sugar plantations dotted the coasts of Brazil and took over Caribbean islands in order to feed Europe's ever-growing sweet tooth. As an industry, sugar was incredibly lucrative, but also labor-intensive and dangerous. Slaves worked in groups in sugarcane fields where snakes and rats roamed. The cane had to be cut at precisely the right time of year, and then bundled and taken to the mill where the cane was crushed through crude rollers, extracting the sweet cane juice. Slaves in the mills had to stoke hot fires as the cane juice was cooked and reduced to a sticky syrup that was then poured into molds where it crystallized into sugar.

African slaves usually built their own communities in Latin American slave societies. New families were created to take the place of families that were uprooted and separated by the voyage across the Atlantic. New religions were formed that combined elements of old traditions from Africa, mixed with the new teachings of Catholicism, and even Native American beliefs. The syncretic religious movements that resulted were uniquely New World in nature, and reflected the needs of the slaves and their new lifestyles. In addition, language proved to be a barrier for slave productivity. The Spanish and Portuguese did not spend excessive time teaching slaves to speak the Iberian languages, and individuals from different areas of Africa did not speak the same languages as each other. New languages or dialects were formed that combined elements from the old, and from Spanish and Portuguese, and over time slaves developed spoken languages that were unique to them and their locations.

The Spanish and Portuguese Crowns designated certain ports as the only locations where slaves could be sold legally in the New World. This was to facilitate recordkeeping, and also to ensure that taxes and duties on slaves reached the royal coffers. In the Spanish Empire, slaves were to be sold in Havana (Cuba), Veracruz (Mexico) and Cartagena (Colombia). In Brazil, slaves were imported to the cities of Recife and Salvador. From these ports, slaves were transported over land or sea to specific plantations and regions throughout Latin America. However, privateers in the black market thrived on the sales of African slaves in other, unofficial locations, and often for better prices. These transactions were not taxed, and the Crowns of Spain and Portugal spent much time, effort, and money trying to eradicate the black market throughout their realms.

Almost from the very beginning, some Europeans questioned the morality of enslaving Africans. One of the most famous dissenters was a Spanish slave-owner turned priest named Bartolomé de las Casas, who argued that Africans and Native Americans were human beings who should not be enslaved or forced to labor for Spanish and Portuguese landowners. One of the key issues for many was the lack of moral foundations upon which the institution of slavery was built. Some of the arguments in support of slavery included the notion that contact between pagan Africans and Christian Europeans was positive because it helped civilize the Africans and led them to live more pious and devoted lives. Another argument in support of slavery was the fact that Spain and Portugal were only continuing a tradition that had been around for thousands of years. Individuals argued that they were not the instigators or creators of slavery, and were in fact simply continuing a practice that was ages old and, furthermore, was sanctioned by the Holy Bible as an acceptable institution. Finally, through religious conversion, slaves' souls were saved, which was of eternally greater significance to them than a few years of discomfort and labor in mortality. In these and other ways, Spain and Portugal justified the practice of slavery and advocated for its continuance in the New World.

African Slavery in Brazil

Brazil was the largest Portuguese colony in the New World. But the Portuguese did not initially find very many things in Brazil that were profitable or valuable. After all, Portugal also had colonies in Africa, India, Asia, and Indonesia, where they made huge profits from trading spices, silk, porcelain, and other luxury items. And, there were other problems with Brazil besides just the monetary ones. It was difficult to entice Portuguese citizens to settle in Brazil. They were content to remain in Portugal, or to travel to the more lucrative colonies in the east. An early attempt to convince wealthy Portuguese landowners to settle in Brazil was set in motion in the early 1500s; large strips of land from the coast to the interior of the continent were created (called "donatary captaincies") and granted to these wealthy individuals. They were supposed to then use their money and influence to settle these areas and make them productive. But again, convincing these Portuguese landowners to actually go to Brazil was a difficult endeavor at best. Another problem was the fact that there were fewer Native American Indians to exploit in Brazil, either for their labor or their gold. If it had not been for the future lucrative sugar industry, the Portuguese might well have left Brazil completely alone after a few years.

But, when it became obvious that sugar was able to compete monetarily with Portugal's eastern empire trade, plans were made to expand the industry all along the Atlantic coastline of Brazil. However, as observed above, using the Native American Indians as a labor force was not a viable option. Therefore the Portuguese began to ship Africans to Brazil from their African colonies. Sugarcane as an industry was introduced to Brazil by the French and Dutch who had been growing it in the Caribbean on small plantations. Brazil's climate and temperature made it an ideal location to grow sugarcane, especially along the coasts in the northern half of the colony. Some of these regions became completely economically dependent on sugar production, and the massive influx of African slaves meant that they made up around 70 percent of the local populations in these areas.

In Brazil, as in other areas of Latin America, slaves were distinguished by their place of birth. A new slave directly from Africa was called a *Boçal*. These slaves were forced to do some of the worst work on the plantations, and they received most of the abuse at the hands of punitive slave-masters. They also underwent significant culture shock as they adjusted to the colonial life, language, work, religious changes, and living conditions in Brazil. On the other hand, a slave that was born in Brazil instead of being born in Africa was called a *Crioulo*. These slaves had several advantages over the Boçales. First of all, they were

Brazilian-born so they did not go through a traumatic ocean voyage that dragged them from their familiar surroundings. Next, they grew up speaking either Portuguese or a local dialect of Portuguese, and therefore were more valuable for some sorts of work because a language barrier did not prevent them from effective communication with masters. Finally, *Crioulos* were occasionally permitted to supervise other slaves, work as house slaves/servants, and work in crafts such as carpentry, masonry, smithing, etc.

When a slave-owner punished or abused recalcitrant slaves, they did have ways of getting revenge or reprisal against their owners, although these methods were sometimes dangerous and could lead to serious retribution by slave-owners. One method employed by Africans in Brazil was to work slowly. When a master complained, the slaved claimed that the lack of food and the poor housing they lived in caused them to be less productive. Sometimes machinery in the sugar mills or tools could "accidentally" break, causing periods of inactivity while the expensive implements and tools were repaired or replaced. Finally, slaves often escaped by just running away. Runaway slaves were called *cimarrones*, and when enough *cimarrones* could gather together in one place in Brazil's interior wilderness, they sometimes established their own communities called *quilombos*. A *quilombo* was simply a settlement comprised of runaway Africans, where they set up African-style "governments" and practiced African-based religions. They often sent out marauding parties to invade nearby Brazilian towns and villages, stole from travelers, freed other slaves, and—on rare occasions—declared war on Portuguese settlements. And like in Africa, there is evidence that slavery was actually practiced in *quilombos*, although not in the same manner as was practiced by the Portuguese on the coasts. African slavery inside *quilombos* was usually never perpetual or hereditary, and slaves were not considered property.

The most famous of the *quilombos* in Brazil was in the state of Pernambuco. This *quilombo* was named Palmares. It was formed around 1600 when the Dutch invaded the northern Brazilian coastline, causing such an uproar that hundreds of slaves were able to escape into the interior while their masters were occupied repelling the Dutch. By the end of the 1600s, Palmares had a population estimated at around 30000 people spread throughout several associated communities. They worked as farmers, artisans, warriors, and they had established their own government. The most famous leader of Palmares was a man named Ganga Zumba, a runaway slave who was supposedly elected to his position by a quasi-democratic election process.

Palmares existed for nearly a century before its final conquest in 1695 by the Brazilian military. Wealthy plantation owners in Pernambuco and the city of Recife funded the military expeditions that were sent out to exterminate the community of runaway slaves. After nearly 20 attempts, the Portuguese were finally successful in capturing a later leader of Palmares named Zumbi, and beheading him in 1695. But even after the demise of Palmares, slaves continued to run away and set up new smaller *quilombos* where they hoped to avoid attracting as much attention. Then, after 1693, the Portuguese in Brazil discovered a rich vein of gold in the territory of Minas Gerais, a region that also was mined for diamonds. This discovery produced a huge gold rush to the southern interior of Brazil, and some of the northern sugar communities, along with the *quilombos*, were abandoned in the quest for easy and instant wealth to the south.

Conclusions

African slavery in the New World was a terrible period in the history of the hemisphere. African peoples were ripped from their homes, families, and ways of life, only to be sent across an ocean and into a harsh life of servitude, punishment, and misery. The African slave trade increased in importance and economic opportunity during the sixteenth, seventeenth, eighteenth, and nineteenth centuries. In the early 1500s, when the slave trade was just beginning to reach the New World, Africans comprised less than 5 percent of all trade across the Atlantic Ocean. But by the early 1800s, slavery had risen to nearly 30 percent of all Atlantic trade. The results for countries in the Caribbean and in South America are still evident to this day.

Filmography

The films on African slavery in Latin America discussed in this chapter include *Quilombo* (1984), a Brazilian film, and *La Última Cena* (*The Last Supper*, 1976), a Cuban film. Both films focus on Latin American slavery in several aspects. But each also has an alternative theme. *Quilombo* uses African slavery as a vehicle for showcasing modern Brazilian music and culture. *La Última Cena* is a piece of Cuban propaganda that comments on the evils of organized religion. In each case, slavery is essential to the narrative, but neither of these films is solely about slavery, but rather about the results of slavery, and the lives of the individuals who were associated with the slave trade in Brazil and the Caribbean.

Quilombo (1984)

The film *Quilombo* (1984) was directed by Carlos Diegues and filmed in Brazil. The film chronicles the history of one of Brazil's most famous and successful runaway-slave cities, Palmares in Pernambuco. The film opens in the year 1650 on a sugarcane plantation, where a Portuguese woman, the matriarch of the plantation, is having a slave punished by having his neck crushed in an apparatus similar to stocks, where his head protrudes through a vice-like set of boards. After this slave's accidental death, the film cuts to the sugarcane fields where a new slave, Ganga Zumba, has just killed an overseer. The slaves in the field decide to seize this opportunity to rise up and they kill a Dutch visitor to the plantation along with his entourage. Afterwards, all the slaves decide to run away to Palmares.

As they travel to Palmares, one of the women gives birth to a son who is named Zumbi, Ganga Zumba's nephew, and a character that is destined for great things later in the movie. The slaves eventually arrive in Palmares and meet the current leader of the city, Acotirene. In a strange exchange, Acotirene proclaims that Ganga Zumba will be the new leader of Palmares. Then she literally disappears and the mantle of leadership falls on Ganga Zumba. These opening scenes set the stage for the rest of the film and the conflicts to follow.

Five years pass and the people of Palmares continue to teach their children the ways of the community and how to survive in the forests. Slave-hunters from the nearby city of Bahia come and attempt to capture some of them. The young child Zumbi is captured and his mother is murdered. He is taken to a monastery, where he is raised by a priest. Zumbi remains in this situation for the next 16 years. After this time has passed, he makes his escape and eventually returns to Palmares where he is welcomed home with gifts and feasts.

The film showcases Brazilian music from the 1980s throughout, and frequently throughout the film the people of Palmares stop what they are doing and sing and dance all day long. There is even a scene where two boys apparently "invent" soccer by kicking a ball with their feet. These cultural references are out of place in a film about Brazilian *quilombos* of the seventeenth century, but director Diegues seems to be using the film as a vehicle for celebrating Brazilian culture. By romanticizing the stories of the past he provides historical legitimacy to much of modern Brazilian society.

Eventually, some of the Portuguese settlers in Brazil decide to declare war on the people of Palmares. They see Palmares as a threat to their slave populations and an incentive for slaves to run away in hopes of arriving at the runaway city. During the war, people are killed on both sides and the fighting continues for many years. Eventually Ganga Zumba travels to the city of Recife, a large sugarcane-based city on the coast, to meet with some of the Portuguese leaders of the colony in hopes of ending the protracted conflict. He is told that if he takes his people to Cucaú (in the interior of the state of Pernambuco, farther away from the sugarcane plantations) they will be left alone and unmolested. Some of the people of Palmares follow Ganga Zumba to Cucaú, but others decide to follow Zumbi, now a young man, who desires to stay and fight against the Portuguese. Eventually, as the Portuguese come to destroy the settlers in Cucaú, Ganga Zumba realizes his mistake, and in order to galvanize support among his followers for a return to Palmares, he commits suicide, making it look like he was poisoned by the Portuguese, and in his dying words encourages his people to return to Palmares and fight with Zumbi.

Eleven years pass, and the Portuguese continue to make plans to march into the mountains and forest to exterminate Palmares. They bring with them cannons and prepare to wipe out the *quilombo* and either kill or recapture its population. After much violence, Palmares is burned and many of the inhabitants are dead. The final blow comes when Zumbi is finally killed, signifying the end of Palmares and the freedom of the runaway slaves.

In *Quilombo*, Diegues discusses concepts such as land ownership and religion. For the people of Palmares, land is communal and everyone shares what they have with everyone else. For the Portuguese, land is owned and worked by specific individuals and others need permission to be there, or they are driven out or killed. In terms of religion, the Brazilian Portuguese are Catholics, while the people of Palmares follow their African religious roots. At one point in the film, when Zumbi manages to escape from the monastery, the priest asks him why he doesn't take his large crucifix with him. Zumbi replies that it served no purpose unless it was turned upside down and used as a sword. Zumbi is responding in this way, signifying that religious indoctrination doesn't always sink in, and rather than being positive for the African slaves, it was actually damaging to their African culture that they were willing to fight to preserve.

Another theme in the film is the way women are portrayed. The Portuguese woman at the beginning of the film who tortures the recalcitrant slave is wearing European-style fashions and sitting in luxury under an umbrella while the punishment takes place. By contrast, the African women are seen as very strong and independent, fulfilling important roles in the community, and are just as physically capable as the men in carrying out their duties.

This film is not a Hollywood production, but instead represents the growing Brazilian film industry. In other words, this film is not a document where Americans are portraying another culture, as in *The Mission*, where Robert De Niro plays a Spanish priest, but instead a piece of cinema, filmed in Portuguese, in which Brazilians portray their own culture and historical past. So, the question is, why would Diegues and the actors desire to portray colonial historical Brazil in this way? The music, dancing, and pride that the film instills in the slave city of Palmares implies that Diegues is portraying Brazil's past slave society, and the blending of both African and Portuguese cultures, in a modern interpretation and context. Whether or not the film can be considered a piece of propaganda—internal or external—is largely irrelevant because it was made for an audience that would appreciate the cultural hat-tipping from both mythology and history to modern Brazilian society in the 1980s.

In 1986, Vincent Canby, writing for the *New York Times*, reviewed *Quilombo* and commented that the film was "colorful and deliberately idealized." Later, in 1992 in the *American Historical Review* (97:4; October, 1992), Augusto Arraes brought the film into contemporary historical context by observing that at the time of *Quilombo*'s release, Brazil was emerging from a 20-year long military dictatorship, and entering into what many hoped would be a period of new political freedoms. In this light, Arraes wrote, "Carlos Diegues . . . made *Quilombo* in order to inspire a utopian vision of Brazil's future." Certainly the past, and particularly the glorifying of past events, can inspire unity and camaraderie in the present because people can relate to their own past as a society, and use the media as a platform to reshape the future of their lives and cultures. *Quilombo* is an example of this type of unification cinema, meant to instill in contemporary Brazilians pride in their past, and their unification as a people and country.

La Última Cena *(1976)*

The first thing to be said about *La Última Cena (The Last Supper*, 1976) is that it is a piece of Cuban propaganda. The film is included in this chapter because of its portrayal of the institution of slavery on a sugar plantation in Cuba in the later 1700s, but its status as propaganda should not be overlooked or forgotten during the viewing. The film was made in Cuba, under the leadership of the Castro regime, and reflects the ideals and notions of that regime on organized religion. Tomás Gutiérrez Alea directed this film, which ultimately proclaims the tragic elements of the slave trade but also elicits a critical response regarding organized religion because of its religious overtones, which merge well with the topics and films discussed in Chapter 8.

The film opens on a sugar mill in the eighteenth century near the city of Havana. A slave has run away, and the overseer of the plantation, Don Manuel, is preparing dogs to track him down. Into this scene comes the Count, the owner of the sugar mill, who seems initially unconcerned about the runaway, saying that it is a matter for the overseer to deal with since it is the overseer's job to keep the mill and plantation running smoothly. Other individuals—slaves and white laborers—occupy the mill, including a priest and the operator of the mill itself who is responsible for the actual process of turning sugarcane into marketable sugar. The slaves assigned to the house wear powdered wigs and pour a bath for the Count while at the same time the mill priest complains about the difficulties he is having teaching the slaves about Christianity.

Later the Count is given a tour of his sugar-making facilities. Tomás Gutiérrez Alea includes this scene to instruct the viewer about the painstaking process of making sugar, and the back-breaking labor that the slaves endure on the plantation. Slaves stir large kettles of cane juice over very hot fires. The method of making sugar is described in detail and, at the end of the process, the white and dark sugar is separated for sale. Interestingly, the sugar mill operator comments to the Count that that which is white must first be black, seemingly indicating that slaves cannot be expected to immediately embrace the customs and religion of Spaniards until they go through a process of refining, much like the arduous task of turning cane juice into dark and then light sugar.

Eventually, the runaway slave is recovered and the overseer, Manuel, who interestingly seems to be a Mulatto himself, cuts of the slave's ear and feeds it to his dogs. The Count is repulsed by this, and the viewer is left with the impression that the Count is out of touch with what goes on at the mill, and that most matters, such as the punishment of runaway slaves, are handled by the overseer, not the Count himself. The development of teaching Christianity to the slaves on the plantation, which has taken place up to this point in the film, culminates in a misbegotten plan by the Count to instruct his slaves about Christianity in a new way. He seems to feel a sense of guilt or uneasiness about the fact that his slaves are not adapting to the new religion rapidly enough and their souls are not saved, and he desires to ease his conscience in this regard. The Count's plan is to perform a reenactment of Christ's Last Supper before his crucifixion. Twelve slaves are selected at random from the group to represent Christ's 12 disciples, including the runaway slave who is selected last.

On Maundy Thursday, the Count sets a huge table with food and wine, and invites the 12 slaves to the table to reenact the Last Supper, with the Count playing the role of Jesus himself. The Count attempts to wash the slave's feet like Christ did with his disciples. This does not go over very well, as the slaves are not used to this sort of treatment and are not sure how to act when the Count attempts to kiss their feet after indiscriminately washing them. Meanwhile, the overseer, Manuel, goes to visit the sugar mill operator, and they talk about how the Count is making them both feel uncomfortable with his queasiness about slave discipline and his ill-conceived attempt to instruct them in the ways of Christianity. They introduce the foreboding idea that the slaves may rise up and rebel as in similar revolutions in Cuba and other Caribbean islands.

As the reenactment of the Last Supper progresses, the Count continues to discuss matters of religion, while the slaves seem more interested in the food

FIGURE 6.1 *La Última Cena* (*The Last Supper*, 1976, Nelson Rodríguez).

and drink. They are uncomfortable at first at the plethora of food on the table, but as the meal progresses they become more comfortable with the feast and partake enthusiastically. But, regarding the Count's discussion of Christianity, the slaves do not comprehend what he is saying to them. At one point, as the Count describes the Eucharist, the slaves act aghast and ask why the people ate Christ. As the meal begins to conclude, the Count has become significantly drunk and the slaves are becoming more and more rowdy, talking in their own languages, telling stories from their own cultures and religions, and drinking more and more wine. The Count drunkenly frees an old man from slavery, and also proclaims that they will not have to do any work on Good Friday.

The following day, a very hungover Count decides it is time to leave the plantation and return to Havana. Having told the 12 slaves that they would not have to work on Good Friday, the slaves are rejoicing and not going to the fields. When Manuel sees this, he is enraged and violently forces them to return to work. The old man who was granted his freedom the previous day is also forced back into the fields to labor. The overseer's heavy-handedness in contrast to the Count's benevolence creates a situation ripe for an uprising. The slaves begin to revolt and they drag the overseer into the middle of the compound and put him in stocks. Then they drag women out of the main house and plan to burn down the entire plantation including the buildings and fields.

While all of this is going on, the priest of the plantation rides to Havana to tell the Count that the overseer is forcing the slaves to return to work. The Count, having returned to a feeling of apathy regarding his slaves and their Christian conversion, washes his hands of the whole thing and says he wants nothing more to do with the situation. As the priest continues to complain, the Count says that sometimes necessary sins are required. However, soon after this conversation, other white residents of the plantation arrive with the news that the slaves have begun a violent revolution. Now the Count is moved to action, and he and the priest gather some other men from Havana who ride back to the mill with weapons in order to put down the insurrection. When they arrive, they find the mill in ruins and one of the white women from the house is dead. In addition, the overseer, Don Manuel, has also been killed by the same slave who ran away at the beginning of the film. In a moment of epiphany, the Count compares the overseer's death with that of Jesus Christ.

As the film concludes, 11 of the 12 "disciples" are found and their heads are cut off and placed on spikes as a reminder of what happens to rebellious slaves. But the twelfth slave, the runaway, cannot be found, and the Count compares him to Jesus' disciple Judas, who was responsible for the death of Christ. The director is implying here that the Don Manuel, who forced the slaves to work on Good Friday, is a symbol for Christ, and the runaway who escaped, compared to Judas, was the only one who was not brought to justice by having his head removed. In other words, organized religion is dangerous and results in death and obstruction, and those who fight against it are only doing what is necessary.

La Última Cena is in itself a parable about the ills of modern religion, told against the backdrop of the institution of slavery on a Cuban sugar plantation. Tomás Gutiérrez Alea makes many comparisons throughout the film, such as the 12 disciples of Christ being slaves, the plantation overseer as a representation of Christ and his death, and the escaped slave as the traitor Judas. In terms of the setting on a sugar plantation, the film does a good job of portraying conditions at sugar mills, and the connections and interactions between slaves and whites. The apparent and confusing about-face of the Count from Maundy Thursday to Good Friday is for the most part inexplicable, but the overall message of the film seems to focus on the ills of organized religion. The historical significance of the film is in its depiction of slave life on sugar plantations, and the trials and abuse they face at the hands of their white masters. And, one can view the film purely from this point of view, and come away with an appreciation of the plight of the slaves on such plantations, while disregarding or turning a blind eye toward the propagandized message that propels the film toward its grisly conclusion.

Further Reading

Bergad, Laird W. *The Cuban Slave Market, 1790–1880*. Cambridge: Cambridge University Press, 2003.

De Queiros Mattoso, Katia M. *To Be A Slave in Brazil: 1550–1888*. New Brunswick, NJ: Rutgers University Press, 1987.

Klein, Herbert S. *African Slavery in Latin America and the Caribbean*. Oxford: Oxford University Press, 2007.

Klein, Herbert S. *The Atlantic Slave Trade*. Cambridge: Cambridge University Press, 2010.

7

REVOLUTIONARY LATIN AMERICA

Republican Government is over-perfect, and it demands political virtues and talents far superior to our own. For the same reason, I reject a monarchy that is part aristocracy and part democracy . . . Do not adopt the best system of government, but the one which is most likely to succeed.

There is no good faith in America, nor among the nations of America. Treaties are only scraps of paper; constitutions are only printed matter; elections, battles, freedom, anarchy, and life are all a torment. America is ungovernable. Those who have served the revolution have plowed the sea.

Simón Bolívar

The Wars for Independence

Revolution and seeking for freedom through revolutionary violence has been endemic in Latin America throughout much of its history. Revolution is a level of rapid change at a basic level, and is usually associated with some sort of violence. In the early decades of the nineteenth century, the colonies in Latin America waged vehement revolutions, both political and social, for freedom from their status as colonies of Spain and Portugal. Indeed, throughout the nineteenth century and into the twentieth, revolutions, motivated by various struggles, would punctuate movements throughout Latin America, from Mexico to Argentina, most of which were fierce and came at the cost of thousands of lives.

Revolutions can be divided into the very broad categories of political and social. Political revolutions use violence to suddenly transform political systems while at the same time trying to not interrupt the underlying structure of society too dramatically. Having said this, some historical political revolutions have not only transformed political systems, they have also significantly altered entire populations through a liberation of some kind.

By contrast, social revolutions are responsible for creating massive changes in the economic and cultural infrastructure of a nation or state. Whereas political revolutions change the structure at the top, social revolutions empower the masses. Also, social revolutions tend to be bloodier and more violent than political revolutions because the masses are involved in securing their new freedoms, and social revolutions are more likely to begin when political revolutions fail or become unstable.

So with this understanding in place, we turn to Latin America in 1810, when political and social revolutions began to set in motion a complete transformation of the entire landscape of the colonies. The results of these movements were widespread and destructive. The emerging wars for independence in Latin America began as political revolutions by groups of *creoles* (individuals of Spanish or Portuguese heritage who were born in the Americas instead of Iberia) who sought to overthrow the power of the *peninsulares* (Spaniards and Portuguese who had been born in Spain or Portugal). These political movements began when creoles began trying to wrest political control of the colonies, cities and entire regions from the colonial powers of Europe. Between 1810 and 1825, social reforms also took place in Latin America, including the end of Indian tribute in some locations, the end of the African slave trade, and the call for an end of political control by Spain and Portugal.

But quickly, the independence movements spun out of control, as Indians, Africans and *Castas* (individuals who were the result of relationships between Spaniards and Indians, Indians and Africans, or Spaniards and Africans) began to rise up and fight both creoles and peninsulares for their own social freedom from cultural, economic, political, and social control. This became one of the most devastating periods of social revolution in modern history. This was not revolution for purely political motives from the top down, but for freedoms from the bottom up. This was social revolution in all its destructive power. The revolutions centered on four distinct areas of Spanish Latin America (Mexico, Venezuela, Argentina, and Peru) and on Portuguese Brazil.

Independence in Mexico

Mexican independence began with a creole priest named Miguel Hidalgo. In 1803 he served as the parish priest in the Mexican town of Dolores, about 100 miles northwest of Mexico City. Dolores was in a predominantly Indian and Mestizo area, and the people who lived there were poor but industrious. Hidalgo was one of a handful of individuals in the area who believed that Mexico should throw off Spanish control and govern itself. After all, if the power of Spain was toppled in Mexico, the creoles, not the peninsulares, would be in control of the country. Hidalgo joined a small clandestine group led by Ignacio Allende, another creole, and they began to discuss their complaints about colonial administration and to plot revolutionary action against the Mexican government. They set a date in December 1810 for their revolution to begin. They hoped to replace peninsular Spanish governors with creole ones, but then to continue to govern Mexico in much the same way it was being governed under Spain; in other words, a classic political revolution.

Their plan moved forward until September 1810, when one of the conspirators leaked information about their plot, forcing the viceroy of Mexico to send troops to Dolores to put down the insurrection. Hidalgo found out about the approaching troops, and he and Allende decided to move the date of their revolution up to September 16, 1810. Father Hidalgo gave his famous proclamation, the *Grito de Dolores* (the Cry of Dolores), in which he called upon his Indian and Mestizo parishioners to rise up and defeat the approaching Spanish troops. Hidalgo hoped to incite a revolution against the leadership of the colony of Mexico. Instead, he unwittingly began a race war that pitted Indians and Mestizos against whites, both creole and peninsular. What Hidalgo hoped would be a quasi-military action to destroy the Spanish government in Mexico turned into a mob that marched to the nearby mining town of Guanajuato, where they proceeded to destroy the town. On September 28, 1810, Hidalgo's 50000 followers killed some 600 Spaniards, and then sacked and burned the town. His movement, much like a boulder rolling down a mountain, continued to gain momentum, as thousands of Indians and Castas joined the cause. Father Hidalgo's status as a priest gave him some control over his growing forces at first, but he eventually lost control of the mob. His goal of restructuring the government failed to translate to the Indian and Mestizo members of his army. The result was not a toppling of the government, but a general fear of Hidalgo's followers by the local populations, which resulted in a lack of true national support for the movement and eventually led to Hidalgo's defeat.

By January 1811, Hidalgo's army was camped near Guadalajara. After losing a major campaign to the Spanish army at the Battle of the Bridge of Calderón (*Batalla del Puente de Calderón*), Hidalgo and Allende fled north hoping to make it across the border of Texas. But they were soon captured and tried for insurrection and treason. On July 30, 1811, Father Hidalgo was defrocked of his priesthood and then shot by a firing squad. The viceroy of Mexico hoped that this would put an end to Hidalgo's movement, but Hidalgo continued to influence the revolution as a martyr instead. Another priest, a Mestizo named José María Morelos, took control of the revolutionary army and led them to Mexico City, where they tried to encircle the capital. But Morelos soon met the same fate as Hidalgo. He was captured, tried, and executed by firing squad on December 22, 1815, meeting the same fate as Father Hidalgo.

Many have wondered at the contribution of Father Hidalgo to Mexico's independence: after all, Hidalgo failed to achieve his goals, and he failed to transform his army into a body determined to topple the colonial government of Mexico. But Mexico celebrates its independence day annually on September 16, the day of Hidalgo's *Grito de Dolores* speech. His legacy was the vision of a free Mexico, and he began the movement that would eventually culminate in the defeat of the colonial Mexican government and Spain's departure from Mexico.

The independence movement that began with Father Hidalgo ended with a narcissistic and ambitious young creole named Agustín de Iturbide. When Hidalgo began his revolution in 1810, Iturbide was an officer in the Spanish military in Mexico City. Between 1816 and 1820 he rose in the ranks and fought a few skirmishes with the revolutionary forces. But in 1820, he set his own plan in motion, a plan that was not driven by a desire for a free and independent Mexico so much as it was a plan for his own personal aggrandizement. In 1820, Iturbide took an army of 25000 Spanish soldiers to fight the rebels. However, once in the field, Iturbide convinced the new leader of the revolutionary forces, Vicente Guerrero, to meet with him in private. During their parley, Iturbide convinced Guerrero that if they were to join their armies together instead of fighting each other, they would be strong enough to topple the government in Mexico City. This would serve both of their purposes. It would free Mexico from domination by the Spanish government, which Guerrero desired, and it would also put Iturbide in a position of political power, which he greatly wanted.

With this plan now accepted, Iturbide drafted a document called the *Plan de Iguala* wherein he promised the people of Mexico that if he were successful in toppling the Spanish Viceroy in Mexico City, he would defend Roman Catholicism as the state religion, he would set up a constitutional monarchy under some well-deserving individual as the new king of Mexico, and he promised the people equality under the law no matter their birthplace, race, or color. Iturbide sent his proclamation throughout central Mexico and gained much support from the people who were tired of Spain's oppressive control. He also seized a caravan of silver from the mining districts destined for Spain, and used the money to recruit more soldiers to his cause. Finally, on February 24, 1821, Iturbide proclaimed Mexican independence. His military forces were far superior to those defending Mexico City, and the viceroy realized he was defeated. On September 27, 1821, Iturbide and the viceroy met, and the viceroy, Juan O'Donojú, signed the Treaty of Córdoba, making Mexico an independent entity from Spain. On July 21, 1822, Iturbide was crowned Agustín I, emperor of Mexico and, like Napoleon had done nearly 20 years earlier in Europe, Iturbide placed the crown of emperorship upon his own head.

Independence in Spanish South America

Independence in Spanish South America followed many elements of the Mexican independence story. South America's period of independence lasted roughly the same amount of time, and also occurred during the same years—between 1810 and the early 1820s. And, as in Mexico, South American independence was instigated and led by men passionate about freedom from Spain who were willing to fight for that freedom. In Spanish South America, two men in particular played a prominent role in freeing various colonies from Spanish control. Simón Bolívar was the larger-than-life personality in the northern part of South America, including Venezuela, Colombia, and Ecuador. In Argentina and Chile, José Francisco de San Martín was the leader who garnered support for independence and achieved significant success.

Bolívar was a creole from Venezuela. He was enamored early on by the power and exploits of Napoleon Bonaparte in Europe. In fact, Bolívar spent time in Europe during the first decade of the 1800s, planning the liberation of Venezuela and gaining support and some financial backing for his plans. By July 1811, Bolívar declared the Spanish government in Venezuela defunct and proclaimed his own independent government there. But several bloody battles had yet to be fought, and between 1811 and 1814 not only did Bolívar's forces fight repeatedly with the Spanish military, but his movement also barely survived a massive earthquake in 1812 that killed thousands of Bolívar's followers and soldiers. In 1814, Bolívar was driven from Venezuela by the Spanish royalist army. He fled to Jamaica and continued to plan Venezuela's independence as an absentee liberator.

By 1816, Bolívar was back in Venezuela with a new army. They fought repeated battles against the Spanish military, which was losing support from the local population and suffering declining morale among the troops. In June 1821, Bolívar finally succeeded in driving the last Spanish army out of Venezuela in the Battle of Carabobo, and declared himself the liberator of Gran Colombia (Venezuela, Colombia, and Ecuador). But he enjoyed less support from the ambivalent local populations than he felt he deserved and, in response to the largely apathetic and lethargic populate of northern South America, Bolívar bitterly marched south to Peru where he hoped to drive the Spanish out as he had done in Gran Colombia.

At this point, our story turns to José Francisco de San Martín. Independence in Argentina followed a different path. In 1806, the British seized the Argentine port of Buenos Aires and opened it to trade with the rest of the British Empire. A lot of money began to flow into the port and the rest of the Argentine colony. But between 1807 and 1810, the people of Argentina drove the English out of the colony, and then revolutionary leader Mariano Moreno announced in 1810 that Argentina would govern itself. Spain was in no position to do anything about this revolutionary proclamation because of political tensions in Spain and the growing insurgency to the north in Mexico and Venezuela. Their forces were stretched too thin, and Argentina was considered too far away to contend with. So Argentina's independence was, for the most part, bloodless.

At this point, the last bastion of major Spanish authority on the South American continent was Peru on the central Pacific coast. In 1814, the Argentine government charged revered military commander José Francisco de San Martín with the task of liberating Peru from Spanish forces. San Martín accepted the commission and quickly decided that the best way to deal with the Spanish in Peru was to first liberate Chile, which lay to the west, over the Andes mountains. So early in 1817, after significant preparations, San Martín marched nearly 5000 troops, thousands of mules, around 1000 horses, and 4000 head of cattle into the Andes mountains en route to Chile. On this brave expedition, San Martín lost of nearly a third of his forces.

San Martín's army entered Chile and, in February 1817, won the Battle of Chacabuco, whereupon he declared Chile independent from Spain. By early 1818, San Martín and a local Chilean military commander named Bernardo O'Higgins had succeeded in driving the rest of Spain's forces from Chile. For the next two years, San Martín built up his forces and prepared for the assault on Peru to the north. It is in Peru that the stories of San Martín and Simón Bolívar converge. Both working for the liberation of Peru at the same time, the two liberators' paths met, and freedom for Spanish South America was at hand.

San Martín and Simón Bolívar had, of course, heard about each other. They decided that their mutual purpose would best be served if they could combine their forces. So they agreed to meet in Ecuador in July 1822 at what came to be known as the Guayaquil Conference to work out the details of their military merger and the final assaults on the royalist forces in Peru. They met for only a few hours on July 26, and then a strange thing happened. Little is known about the private meeting and no documentation has survived the encounter. But what is known is that Bolívar and San Martín could not agree on the type of government that should be instituted in Peru following its independence. At the conclusion of the meeting, Bolívar announced that he would personally lead the combined military force against Spanish Peru, and San Martín announced that he would return to Argentina and then go into retirement in Europe, where he remained for the rest of his life. Historians speculate that Bolívar wanted to set up a republican government in Peru, whereas San Martín desired a monarchy. At the conclusion of the meeting the two decided to part company, and this set the stage for the final assault on the forces of Spain in South America.

Bolívar tool the large military force and by 1824, after a series of bloody skirmishes, managed to defeat the last Spanish forces in South America at the Battle of Ayacucho. Spanish South America was finally liberated from Spain's control, leaving Spain with a few Caribbean islands as the only remaining vestige of their once mighty New World empire. In 1825, Bolívar divided the Peruvian colony into two halves, naming the southern portion Bolivia, after himself, and the northern half Peru. Then he returned to Gran Colombia, only to find it in political chaos and fragmenting into three separate nations. Bitter at the dissolution of Gran Colombia and his loss of authority there, Bolívar attempted to proclaim himself the dictator of the region. But after severe resistance by the people, he resigned his authority and prepared to go into European exile in

April 1830. But before he could leave Venezuela, he died of tuberculosis. On his deathbed, disillusioned and frustrated, he proclaimed that "those who have served the revolution have plowed the sea."

Independence in Brazil

The push for independence in Brazil was very different than in Spanish-speaking Latin America. Where the Spanish Latin American revolutions had been drawn out, violent, and racial, the revolution in Brazil was quick, bloodless, and very politically motivated. In 1807, in Europe, Napoleon demanded that Portugal break its economic alliance with Britain. Napoleon already had control of Spain, having captured the royal family and installed his brother Joseph Bonaparte on the Spanish throne. Portugal refused to sever its ties with Britain and, as a result, Napoleon prepared to invade Portugal by marching troops through Spain.

In order to prevent Napoleon from capturing the royal family in Lisbon, the Portuguese royal court began preparing for a massive migration. They decided that if the Portuguese Crown was not in Portugal when Napoleon arrived, then his conquest would be meaningless. They decided to decamp to Brazil. Sailing on both Portuguese and British ships, the Portuguese queen, Maria I, along with the prince regent Dom João, and the entire royal family, escaped to Brazil where they continued to rule the Portuguese Empire. Along with the royal family, others escaped to Brazil as well, including the council of state, the royal ministers and advisors, the high court, the treasury, the military commanders (generals and admirals), the hierarchy of the Church, servants, functionaries, businessmen, courtiers, and some important Portuguese citizens. All told, the number of people who left Portugal in November 1807 totaled nearly 15000 people, sailing in more than 50 vessels. They also took with them the entire Portuguese treasury, government files, a printing press (which would be Brazil's first), and several libraries. Such a massive migration of state officials and dignitaries had never before occurred in European history.

They landed in Bahia, Brazil in January 1808 and then sailed on to Rio de Janeiro, where they set up the new capital of the Portuguese Empire. All of a sudden Brazil became a very important place. Some immediate effects of the migration included the creation of schools, libraries, a printing house, banks, universities and medical schools, and the influx of thousands of Europeans who brought with them European culture, style, and a certain *je ne sais quoi* that was missing from Brazil before their arrival. In addition, the political effects were staggering. Never before in Latin American history had a monarch visited a colony, let along moved there. Now, the world had to come to Rio when they wanted to interact with the Portuguese Crown. Brazil began to change economically as well. The ports were opened to the empire for trade. Brazil was no longer considered a colony, but an equal kingdom with Portugal. Mercantilism, whereby Brazilian commodities were harvested or mined, and then shipped back to Portugal, was now stopped as these resources stayed in Brazil. Brazil also began manufacturing and became more economically self-sufficient.

But these benefits also came with new problems for the former colony. Brazilian-born governors and functionaries in political and ecclesiastical offices were in many cases replaced by officials from Portugal. During the early 1800s, Portugal began to feel pressure from Britain to abolish its slave trade as well, but Brazil continued to utilize slavery as an institution until the end of the century. In addition, many Brazilians and Portuguese in Brazil began to wonder why they needed to maintain their relationship with Portugal at all. After all, they were very self-sufficient and had little use for a "mother country" across the ocean that was effectively under the control of Napoleon.

In 1814, Queen Maria I died and João VI was crowned king of the Portuguese Empire. Then, in 1815, Napoleon Bonaparte was defeated in Europe and banished from the continent, giving Portugal and Spain their liberty once again. Now, the Portuguese political leadership who had remained behind in Portugal began to demand that João return to Lisbon and leave Rio behind. They advocated for returning Brazil to colonial status and stepping back into the old mercantilist relationship that existed before Napoleon's invasion and the flight of the Portuguese royalty. The problem was that João didn't want to leave Brazil and Brazil didn't want him to leave. But when he initially refused to return, the Portuguese leaders in Lisbon began to draw up plans to abolish the monarchy in the Portuguese Empire, and transition into a republican form of government. João realized that he had to choose; either he could return to Portugal and run the risk of Brazil declaring itself independent rather than revert back to colonial status; or he could remain in Brazil and lose his status as the king of the Portuguese Empire. João then came up with a scheme that would allow him to retain his crown and not lose Brazil, even if Brazil did declare its independence from Portugal. In 1821, he finally returned to Portugal with several thousand members of the royal court, ministers, and others, although the majority of those who had gone to Brazil nearly 15 years earlier remained behind. But, when he returned to Portugal, he did not take his son, Crown Prince Dom Pedro, with him. He left Pedro behind as the viceroy of Brazil. And he probably gave his son instructions to declare Brazil an independent country if the Portuguese court threatened to return Brazil to colonial status.

As João predicted, when he returned, the Portuguese nobility were furious that Dom Pedro had not returned with his father. They began the process of restoring Brazil's colonial standing, and they sent a letter to Brazil demanding that Dom Pedro also return immediately to Portugal and take his place as the heir to the throne. But on September 7, 1822, Dom Pedro issued his famous declaration where he stated, "Eu fico!" (I remain). This statement later became known as the *Grito do Ipiranga* (Ipiranga was the name of a small river near the city of São Paulo) and signified Brazil's declaration of independence from Portugal. And that's it. There were a few minor revolts in northern Brazil, but nothing that could compare with the violence and bloodshed in Spanish Latin America. There was very little political, economic, or social disruption. After all, the apparatus of state remained in place under Pedro, now Pedro I of Brazil. Brazil remained a monarchical government until 1889, when it shifted to a republic. They didn't need to create a new political system because they already had one in place that functioned well and provided stability to the people of Brazil. In addition, unlike in Spanish Latin America, there was no territorial fragmentation in Brazil as had occurred in the rest of Latin America. Instead of separating into many different countries, Brazil remained one single nation under one ruler.

The Post-Independence Revolutionary Period

Latin Americans fought hard for their freedom from Iberian control. Between 1810 and 1825 the colonies won victories, set up governments, and divided into new countries. But independence didn't fix all of their problems. Some of these areas continued to struggle for years. They discovered that even though they had fought for their freedom from political and economic oppression by Spain and Portugal, they were fettered by many of the same political and economic problems that they had endured under colonialism such as governmental corruption, racial inequality, and economic exploitation. And so the revolutions continued. Latin American peoples believed that if they continued to fight, they would one day find that elusive freedom they were seeking. Speaking about a nineteenth-century revolution in Nicaragua, author Albert Carr stated:

> To most . . . people it seemed that the difficulties of their lives could only be made worse by radical change . . . They were not in favor of anything; they were merely against everything; their attitude might be described as anti-ism. They would follow a revolutionary leader to help him destroy an oppressive government, but as soon as the new government was established, it in turn became their enemy for it represented the hated power of the law.
>
> *(Carr 1975: 166)*

This statement reflects the difficulties that Latin American peoples and leaders faced in the century after independence. They knew they wanted something different, something better. But how to achieve that change was perpetually beyond their grasp. So they continued to fight and die.

Mexico

Mexico provides a prime example. Between 1821 and 1921, Mexico floundered politically and economically. It had liberated itself from Spain but nothing really changed. Military dictators ruled the nation in much the same way Spain did, and for Indians and Mestizos, life continued to be very difficult. In 1876, military dictator Porfirio Díaz took power in a classic military *coup d'état*. He remained in power until he was forced out of office in 1911. While in power, he rapidly modernized Mexico but he also treated the poor so badly that they needed relief from his oppressive methods. In 1910, the frustrated populace began a revolution to topple the government. The Mexican Revolution, as it has come to be called, has been described as the first of the great twentieth-century revolutions, predating the other massive revolutionary movements in Russia, China, Cuba, and Iran, to name a few.

In 1911 in southern Mexico, the revolutionary Emiliano Zapata raised an army to fight for land rights of the villagers in his area. When their constitutional rights were trampled by the Mexican government, Zapata revolted against the Díaz regime and he continued to fight for nearly a decade. At the same time in northern Mexico, Francisco "Pancho" Villa was doing roughly the same thing, fighting against the government for a small group of farmers and ranchers. Both Villa and Zapata were successful for a while at keeping government troops at bay, and they even toppled the government of Mexico at one point, ruling briefly before returning to their homelands and peoples to avoid the temptations of government power that they were fighting against. Both were eventually assassinated—Zapata in 1919 and Villa in 1923—and Mexico attempted to return to a tentative peace under President Álvaro Obregón. But the revolutionary movements continued until the latter half of the twentieth century.

Cuba

The island nation of Cuba also experienced revolutionary violence, and as a result of the Cuban Revolution of the 1950s, Fidel Castro came to power and created a communist dictatorship on the island. Castro was born in 1926 and attended a Catholic boarding school in his youth. In 1945 he entered law school and began to become active in political revolutionary activities in Cuba, Colombia, and other locations in the Caribbean. After graduation from law school, he eventually decided to enter politics, but former Cuban dictator Fulgencio Batista returned to Cuba from retirement in Florida and orchestrated a military coup that toppled the Cuban government in 1952. Batista took absolute power, threw out the Cuban constitution, and dissolved the congress. Castro believed that his chances for entering into Cuban politics at this point were narrow indeed, and he realized that there was no chance for political reform in Cuba now. He soon came to the conclusion that the only way to change the political climate in Cuba was through revolution.

In July 1953, Castro led an attack on an army barracks in Cuba. Many of his followers were killed in the attack, and Castro himself was captured and arrested. After his trial, he was sentenced to 15 years in prison. But in an act of clemency, Batista commuted his sentence and allowed him to leave prison after serving only a few months. Castro immediately fled to Mexico, where he began plans for the violent overthrow of Batista's government. Also while in Mexico, Castro met another Latin American revolutionary, Ernesto "Che" Guevara, who would become Castro's accomplice in the growing Cuban revolution.

Castro and Guevara returned to Cuba in December 1956 and began a guerrilla campaign in the Sierra Maestra mountains of eastern Cuba. Support from the rural population in the countryside aided Castro in many victories over the Cuban military troops sent to stop him. Over the next three years, Castro's revolution continued to gain momentum and the Batista regime continued to lose support. Many of Batista's troops began to defect to Castro's camp, and by November 1958, Batista realized that he was defeated. So in a desperate move, Batista fled to the Dominican Republic, leaving Cuba open for Castro to take up control.

Castro assumed political power in January 1959. He started changing Cuba's political and economic structure. Castro nationalized Cuban farmland, expropriated US property in Cuba, including several sugarcane plantations, and in 1961 publically announced that he was instituting a Marxist-communist government for Cuba. Eventually, tensions between Castro's Cuba and the United States culminated in the Bay of Pigs invasion (1961) and the Cuban Missile Crisis (1962). Like the Mexican Revolution, the Cuban Revolution led to significant social and political change in Cuba, and resulted in the long-term leadership of Fidel Castro, who led Cuba from 1959 until his self-imposed retirement in 2008. In terms of longevity, Castro ruled Cuba during the presidencies of no less than ten US presidents, spanning from Eisenhower to George W. Bush.

Conclusions

Whether rapid or measured, fierce or vicious, political or social, revolutions have been an important part of Latin America's history. And many more Latin American countries than those discussed in this chapter have experienced one or more revolutions in their history, countries such as Nicaragua, El Salvador, Argentina, Chile, Brazil, and Peru to name a few. It could be argued that revolution has been endemic in Latin America during its history since the beginning of the nineteenth century. But on a few rare occasions, revolutions in Latin America have eventually brought more positive change, and while most of Latin America's revolutions have caused much disorder, passion, and carnage, some have eventually brought about positive changes in their respective countries. And it should be remembered that Latin America is not the only region on earth where revolution has been used as a tool for change, both politically and socially. Countries in Africa, Asia, Europe, and the Middle East have all had their share of conflict, both domestic and inter-regional. As long as we as humans disagree about the way government and society should be, and as long as we become disenchanted with the status quo, revolution will remain a part of history that cannot be ignored.

Filmography

The three films discussed below all focus on aspects of revolutionary violence in Latin America. Unfortunately, no films exist that chronicle the independence movements of the early 1800s. But *¡Viva Zapata!* (1952), *Burn!* (1969), and *Che* (2008) all showcase the revolutionary spirit that has been present in Latin America almost since its inception. Each of these films portrays the struggle for freedom that has existed in Latin America throughout its history; from the conquest, through the colonial period, and during the twentieth century and beyond. This reality is described poignantly in the film *Burn!* As José Dolores, a would-be revolutionary, tells William Walker, a British businessman and mercenary, that if someone gives you freedom, it is not freedom. Freedom is something you take.

¡Viva Zapata! *(1952)*

¡Viva Zapata! was released in 1952, directed by Elia Kazan, based on a screenplay by John Steinbeck. The film details the revolutionary life of Emiliano Zapata who dedicated his adult life to fighting against corrupt leaders in Mexico. The film opens in Mexico City in 1909, just a couple of years prior to the ousting of the Mexican dictator Porfirio Díaz. A group of *campesinos*, or poor farmers, have come to Díaz to protest the taking of their farmland by wealthy landowners in the area. Díaz is con-committal and dismisses the group after only a few taciturn words. At this point one of the *campesinos*, Emiliano Zapata, protests that they cannot wait for Díaz's promised restitution, because they need to grow their corn now, during the growing season. Díaz gets annoyed and marks Zapata's name on a sheet of paper naming all of the visiting *campesinos*. This opening scene sets the stage for the conflict between Zapata and the Mexican government throughout the rest of the film.

Back in the countryside, the *campesinos*, following Zapata's lead, cross into the contested land that has been confiscated from them. Immediately armed guards arrive on horseback and shoot at the poor farmers, and after killing one of the guards, Zapata is forced to go into hiding. He is soon found by a man named Fernando Aguirre who is not historical, but rather a literary device invented by writer John Steinbeck. Throughout the film, Aguirre represents political power, national progress, and, above all, greed. At one point in the film, Aguirre states that he is a friend to no one, only logic.

From Aguirre, Zapata learns about a political dissenter, Francisco Madero, who is running a campaign to oust Díaz from power. Zapata is interested in Madero's cause, but is forced to deal with more pressing local matters having to do with his people and their lack of food. As Zapata continues to fight against government oppression in Mexico, Madero gains ground in the north and eventually meets Zapata and grants him the military rank of general.

In due course, Díaz is ousted and Madero becomes president of Mexico. Madero desires to reward Zapata for his role in the fighting by granting him a ranch. Zapata refuses and wants to know when Madero will give the *campesinos* their land back. Madero refuses and instead asks Zapata to have his soldiers stack their weapons. Reluctantly, Zapata agrees to relinquish their arms, thinking it will be a step toward getting his people their land back. But when Zapata's men give up their weapons, President Madero's ranking military commander, General Victoriano Huerta, brings in troops to kill Zapata and his followers. Huerta comments that Zapata must be killed because he believes in what he is fighting for. Zapata escapes, and once again flees to the hills to continue his fight, now against the government of Madero.

Not long after Zapata's escape, General Huerta, who is now supported by Aguirre, the man who represents ultimate government power, kidnaps President

FIGURE 7.1 Marlon Brando as Zapata in *¡Viva Zapata!* (1952, 20th Century Fox).

Madero and has him assassinated. Huerta then declares himself the new president of Mexico. At this juncture, Zapata teams up with northern revolutionary Francisco "Pancho" Villa. Together they eventually defeat Huerta and decide that Zapata will be the new president of Mexico. Steinbeck now writes into the narrative an ironic scene where President Zapata is visited in Díaz's former office by a group of his own *campesinos* who still need help getting their land back. Zapata reluctantly refuses, stating that it is more difficult to restore the land now that he is in charge of all of Mexico because there are more pressing matters he must attend to. But he realizes what power does to all men, and decides to leave with the *campesino* and abandon the presidency to help them right their situation. Aguirre, who has now turned his allegiance to Zapata because of his presidential power, tells Zapata not to go, but Zapata refuses to be corrupted by political power and leaves with his followers.

Zapata returns home to discover that his brother, Eufemio, has taken some land by force and driven the rightful owners away. Eufemio tells Zapata that all the time they spent being revolutionaries and fighting corruption never made him any richer, and he wants to take what he desires now. Zapata confronts his brother and Eufemio is shot in the ensuing argument. Zapata realizes that a little power can corrupt even the best of men.

In Mexico City, the new president of Mexico, Venustiano Carranza, advised by Aguirre, decides that in order to stop the revolutionary violence in Mexico, he needs to have Zapata killed. Aguirre and Carranza ruminate on the difficulty of killing an idea, and the fact that Zapata has become more than a man, and is now a symbol for freedom. Working with the military, Carranza sets a trap for Zapata, an unguarded supply center of weapons and ammunition. When Zapata goes to inspect the arms, he is shot and killed. But Steinbeck leaves the viewer with the powerful admonition that sometimes a dead man can be a terrible enemy, meaning that Zapata's revolutionary ideals will live on without him.

¡Viva Zapata! portrays the quintessential revolutionary figure, fighting against the status quo and trying to create a better world. And just like Bolívar, San Martín, and Hidalgo, Zapata became a symbol for freedom and justice in the face of political corruption and exploitative power. Zapata had the chance to wield this power from the president's office but, fearing his own imperfections as a mortal man, he chose to leave this opportunity behind and continue to fight for freedom from a position that he understood, on the side of the poor and oppressed, and he gave his live for their eventual independence from political exploitation.

Burn! *(1969)*

Burn! was released in 1969, an Italian film directed by Gillo Pontecorvo. The film recounts the story of a fictional character named Sir William Walker, a British entrepreneur and mercenary who has been sent by the British government to a small Portuguese sugar-producing island in the Caribbean named Queimada. Even though the character William Walker in *Burn!* is fictitious, he represents the revolutionary zeal that drove the historical William Walker, an American filibuster, in his attempts to conquer and rule Nicaragua in the 1850s.

In *Burn!*, Walker is sent by the British to the Portuguese island of Queimada to create a disturbance that will disrupt the flow of sugar from the island, prompting a response by the British military to gain control of the island and its sugar industry. The island's name, Queimada, means "burned" in Portuguese, signifying the importance of the burning of the sugarcane fields on the island during the encroaching insurrection by the slave population. The island colony supports fewer than 5000 whites, with the black slave population dominating the population of the island. As Walker arrives, the Portuguese officials are carrying out an execution on a man named Santiago who led an unsuccessful rebellion among some of the slaves. Because that revolution failed, Walker begins to instigate another revolution among the black population.

Walker approaches a slaved named José Dolores who he believes would make a good revolutionary leader. Walker's plan calls for Dolores and his followers to rob the bank in the city and to take the gold to their village on the other side of the island. Then Walker begins playing both sides against each other. He informs the Portuguese officials that he has discovered the stolen gold in a small village in another part of the island. The Portuguese prepare to march troops to the village. Then Walker travels to the village to bring the revolutionaries weapons with which to defend themselves. When the confrontation comes, the villagers defeat the soldiers and celebrate their victory and growing revolution.

As the insurrection grows in the countryside, Walker suggests that the Portuguese put down the violence as quickly as possible. If the rebels get too powerful, it might result in a disastrous revolution like the slave revolt that took place in Haiti between 1791 and 1794. In the Haitian Revolution, a massive uprising on the island resulted in the massacre of thousands of white Europeans, and control of Haiti going to the former slaves. Walker also instigates the assassination of the Portuguese governor of Queimada. In the violence that ensues, the Portuguese leaders abandon the island and British warships take up positions along the island's coasts. In this destabilized situation, José Dolores desires to discuss the relationship between the black and white peoples on the island with Walker. Soon, the new white leadership of the island abolishes slavery in Queimada. But Dolores is not pleased that he is not included in the island's new leadership. The new British governor tries to convince Dolores that he and his followers need to continue to harvest the sugarcane so that the island's economy can continue to prosper. After some debate, Dolores agrees that the black population will go back to the plantations as free men but the white leaders of the island should no longer treat them poorly; the threat of another revolution is herein implied.

When we next see Walker, ten years have passed. Walker has become a recluse and is shunned from polite society. He now lives back in England, but on his own without recognition of the work he did ten years earlier on Queimada. But he is eventually contacted by a representative of the London Stock Exchange who wants to increase revenue from the sugar industry on Queimada. The sugar revenue had fallen off due to increased violence and newly emerging revolutionary activity in the area, and the bankers were eager to see it increase again. Walker agrees to return to the island as a military advisor and to quell the new rebellion led by José Dolores. The irony is that Walker was instrumental in starting the revolution on Queimada in the first place. Now he returns to the island to bring an end to the revolution that he instigated ten years earlier.

When Walker arrives, his first order of business is to convince Dolores to end the violence. When Dolores reacts harshly to Walker's return, Walker decides that more drastic measures need to be taken to stop the revolution. Because much of Dolores' support comes from small villages in the countryside, Walker orders the villages vacated and burned. Huge tracts of the jungle are burned and the villagers are rounded up with increasing levels of violence on the part of the British soldiers. As more of the island goes up in flames, the government decides that Walker's presence is too provocative and tries to expel him from the island. Instead, Walker orchestrates a coup that ousts the governor of Queimada. Walker then decides that burning the villages and jungles is not enough, and he orders that the sugarcane fields should also be burned. Dolores' fighters were using the cane fields as hiding places and as they retreated from the burning fields, they were shot by soldiers. Government officials on Queimada become concerned that the burning of the cane fields will surely diminish the economic output of the island.

Eventually, José Dolores is captured by the British, who plan to put him to death. However, Walker argues that it might be more dangerous in the long run to kill him and make him a martyr and a myth. But when they offer Dolores his life in exchange for exile, he declines. The film ends with the soldiers constructing a gallows on which to hang Dolores, and Walker prepares to leave Queimada once again. But in an ultimate irony, as Dolores is hanged and dies, Walker, while walking to the ship that will carry him back to England, is stabbed to death by a black porter.

The significance of the film *Burn!* is that it displays the power of revolution in a small enclave of Latin America, and represents revolutions that took place all over the region. Dolores characterizes the oppressed population who fight for a better life, and Walker epitomizes the corrupt governmental power that fights to keep the population overworked and defeated. In this way, Walker and Aguirre in *¡Viva Zapata!* play similar roles, representing the corrupt nature of power, and the violence that it ultimately instigates. And while *Burn!* is fictional, it embodies many of the same issues that are to be found in historical revolutions throughout Latin America in the nineteenth and twentieth centuries.

Che *(2008)*

In 2008, director Steven Soderbergh released two films portraying the revolutionary life of Ernesto "Che" Guevara. The films were austerely titled *Che Part One: The Argentine*, and *Che Part Two: Guerrilla*. In *The Argentine*, Che's involvement with Fidel Castro and the Cuban Revolution is portrayed from Che's perspective. In *Guerrilla*, Che leaves Cuba with a small group of fighters, and lands in Bolivia where he hopes to carry out a revolution similar to the one in Cuba. Although *Guerrilla* is not included in this chapter, nevertheless the two films together portray Latin American revolutionary violence in the latter half of the twentieth century, and they chronicle the life and death of one of Latin America's greatest revolutionary leaders.

The Argentine opens in Havana, Cuba in 1964, following the successful Cuban Revolution that brought Fidel Castro to power. The plot device of an interview serves as a grounding device throughout the film, as a series of flashbacks punctuate the progression of the story. In one such flashback, Che delivers a speech at the United Nations in 1964. He condemns US imperialism and defends the rights of Cubans to be free from the economic hegemony of the United States.

The film the moves back to Mexico City in 1955, where a group of revolutionaries, including Fidel Castro, meet to plan the Cuban coup. Che (played by Benicio del Toro) participates in the meeting and meets Castro for the first time. Castro describes the relationship between Cuba and the United States as one of neocolonial economic control, and says that he plans to break that bond.

The following year, Castro, Che, and around 80 other men sail from Mexico to Cuba to begin the revolution. They land on the southeast side of the island and immediately engage government troops. Of the 80 men who arrived with Castro, less than 20 survive the first encounter. Now, Castro's men must survive in the jungle while petitioning the local villagers to support them in their cause of toppling the government led by the dictator Fulgencio Batista.

Che's character and personality are developed throughout the film, including his health concerns with asthma, and his insecurity stemming from the fact that he is Argentinean, not Cuban. At the beginning, Che travels with the men and acts as a physician when needed (Che earned a medical doctor's degree in Argentina in 1953). As they travel through the Cuban countryside, more and more poor Cubans join their movement and support them with food and other supplies. Some of the young men join Castro's army as well, but as the numbers grow, so do discipline problems. Some of Castro's men steal money and rape women, and kill some villagers and burn down their homes and other buildings. When the actions of these men are discovered, they are executed as an example that this kind of behavior would not be tolerated by Castro, Che, and the other revolutionary leaders.

After much time marching through the mountainous jungles of eastern Cuba, Castro promotes Che to the rank of *comandante*. Now that Che has more authority than before, he begins to display more confidence and demonstrates more leadership qualities. Interestingly, as Che marches with his men through the rough terrain, he carries books with him to read and study during periods of rest. He also kept meticulous journals chronicling his movements and the events of the revolution. He encouraged his soldiers to study as well, especially reading and math as he felt these were important skills for the men to have after the revolution succeeded. As time moves on, Castro's confidence in Che's leadership grows, and Castro places Che in charge of training new recruits.

Eventually, Castro tasks Che with holding the center of the island and uniting all the isolated factions and independent revolutionaries. Che carries out this assignment with much success and the revolutionary army continues to take towns and villages, and gain the support of more and more people. Che does a lot of motivational speaking to keep morale up. He talks of the revolution as not just an isolated event in Cuba, but as an international conflict between the wealthy and the poor. In many cases, Che's persuasive speeches seem to be wasted on his listeners because they don't have the educational background that he has and cannot internalize his words completely, but they recognize his passion and become more and more loyal to him and his mission to aid Castro in the Cuban Revolution.

As Castro's army gains more ground and begins to approach Havana, Batista begins to panic. One of the last major cities between Castro's forces and Havana is the city of Santa Clara. Batista's soldiers put up a very strong fight, killing many of Castro's men. But ultimately, Castro's army overruns the city and begins the march to Havana. When Batista realizes he has lost the country, he flees the island, thus preparing Castro for his arrival in Havana as a hero and liberator.

Che Guevara is arguably the most well-known revolutionary fighter in Latin American history. In fact, Che has become something of a symbol of rebellion today as people purchase T-shirts, posters, and bumper stickers of Che without really knowing or understanding anything about him or what he fought for. Like other revolutionaries before him, he fought for freedom against oppression. His fight was not an overt contest against colonialism as many revolutions in Latin America had been before him. Rather his fight was ideological and his goals were to liberate Latin Americans from tyranny, economic domination, and the powerful political and economic hegemony of the United States, Great Britain, and other powerful world powers in the latter half of the twentieth century. To this end, following the Cuban Revolution, Che traveled to Africa and other countries in South America attempting to spread his revolutionary message. Ultimately, Che was captured and killed in Bolivia while attempting to carry out a revolution similar to the one in Cuba. When the time came for his death, his executioner faltered and could not pull the trigger. Che remarked, "Shoot me, you coward! You are only going to kill a man!" (Anderson 1997: 739).

In his last moments of life, Che understood that even if the revolutionary leader dies, the revolution lives on and is carried forward by new leaders that rise up to take the place of the fallen.

Further Reading

Anderson, Jon Lee. *Che Guevara: A Revolutionary Life*. New York: Grove Press, 1997.

Carr, Albert. *The World and William Walker*. Santa Barbara, CA: Praeger, 1975.

Galeano, Eduardo. *Open Veins of Latin America*. New York: Monthly Review Press, 1997.

Gonzales, Michael J. *The Mexican Revolution*. Albuquerque, NM: University of New Mexico Press, 2002.

Guevara, Ernesto Che. *Guerrilla Warfare*. New York: BN Publishing, 2007.

Harvey, Robert. *Liberators: Latin America's Struggle for Independence*. New York: Overlook Press, 2002.

Wicklam-Crowley, Timothy P. *Guerrillas and Revolution in Latin America*. Princeton, NJ: Princeton University Press, 1993.

8

RELIGION IN LATIN AMERICA

Don't you know, priests, why our sermons do not touch the people's heart? Because we do not preach to the eyes, only to the ears.

Father António de Vieira

I believed, when I entered this convent, I was escaping from myself, but alas, poor me, I brought myself with me!

Sor Juana Inés de la Cruz

Religion in Colonial Latin America

Religion as an institution has historically provided unity of belief, and social unity as well in world communities. In Latin America, Roman Catholicism was introduced into Indian communities in the late 1400s and early 1500s. Within a century, Catholicism was firmly implanted along the coasts, in pockets in the interior, in towns, on islands, among peasants and elites alike. Religion in Latin America can be viewed in two separate time periods, colonial and postcolonial.

During the colonial period in Latin American history (1492–1825), the work of the Church was divided between the secular and regular clergy. The secular clergy worked in the cities and towns, ministered to the parishes, and participated in the politics and economic activities in the colonies. In some situations the secular clergy also worked in rural areas or on plantations. By contrast, the *regular* clergy were what some would think of as missionaries. They spent their time in the more sparsely inhabited regions of the New World, among Native Americans in extremely rural areas. Their principal task was to convert Indians to Christianity, teach and catechize them, and instruct them in the doctrines of the Church. They were also instrumental in imparting the fundamentals of European culture, languages, and education. Both groups represented the authority of the Church and the pope, but the way they went about their work was significantly different. Whereas the regular clergy lived among native villagers, learned to speak their languages, and tried to save their souls, the secular clergy opted for representing the Church to Spaniards and Portuguese in the cities and urban areas, focusing on the ordinances and public presence of the Church among European settlers.

In addition, there was the potential for conflict between the two groups over jurisdictions. When the distinction between "civilized" and "uncivilized" was clear, there was less room for contention. But when Indian settlements under the direction of the regular clergy began to grow and attract Spanish and Portuguese settlers, secular priests came along and both sides of the clergy argued that the jurisdiction belonged to them: the secular because they were required to oversee the work of the Church in the towns, villages, and cities; the regular because they had been there from the beginning and didn't want to just walk away from their parishioners and converts.

The roles of the Church and politics in society were usually combined in some way. In the early 1500s, the pope granted to the monarchs of Spain enormous power over the dealings of the Church within the Spanish Empire. This papal document was called the *Patronato Real*, or Royal Patronage. This document was specifically granted to Ferdinand and Isabella because of their zeal and ardor in sustaining and doing the work of the Church in Spain and its territories. The *Patronato Real* gave the Catholic monarchs—as they were called—the authority to appoint priests and bishops, disseminate papal bulls and decrees, and collect tithes and offerings for use within the empire. This authority transferred over to Spanish viceroys in Latin America who had tremendous control over the workings of both Church and state.

Finally, one of the important aspects of the Catholic Church in this time period was the Inquisition. Initially, the Inquisition was an instrument used by the monarchs of Spain and other European countries to ensure purity and the absence of heresy in the Church. Prior to Columbus' voyage across the Atlantic Ocean, Isabella had issued a decree ordering that all Jews and Muslims in Spain either convert to Catholicism or leave the kingdom. And while many did actually leave Spain, many more chose to remain and convert to Christianity. The problem was that the new converts sometimes had the tendency to backslide or to convert in name only, and carry out the outward actions without changing their actual beliefs. So, the Inquisition was used to ensure that conversion was indeed real, and that the new Christians were influenced enough that even if their conversions were for less than pure ecclesiastical reasons, they never indicated anything to the contrary in their actions or words.

The Church used the Inquisition in Latin America throughout the colonial period, but the torture and violence that permeated the Spanish Inquisition of the 1400s and 1500s was not as prevalent in Latin America as it had been in Spain. The most widespread punishments in Latin American colonies for those convicted of heresy or other ecclesiastical crimes were loss of property, imprisonment, beatings, and other public humiliations. Most convictions were for offenses such as blasphemy, bigamy, homosexuality, moral degeneration, and other similar offenses. It is estimated that fewer than 100 persons were condemned to death by the Inquisition during the colonial period in Latin American history.

Religion in Modern Latin America

After 1825, the newly emerging states of Latin America that had just won their freedom from Spanish and Portuguese authority retained many of the ecclesiastical traditions that had been so prevalent throughout the 300 years of colonial rule. The Roman Catholic Church remained the most important religious institution in the hemisphere, and it also permeated the political and social realms of the new countries as well. However, during the latter half of the nineteenth century, the new nations of Latin America also began to interact more closely with other European countries, and also with the United States. And while Roman Catholicism remained fully entrenched in Latin American communities, other faiths began to appear. Through the work of Protestant religious missionaries, other evangelical religious movements began to take hold in some communities, and denominations such as the Presbyterians and Methodists formed religious communities within Latin American cities.

Like the Protestant Reformation of the 1500s in Europe, Latin America began a process of limited religious reformation as well. And as in Europe, the Catholic Church in Latin America also underwent a transformation similar to the Counter-Reformation of sixteenth-century Europe. The Catholic Church was placed in an awkward position following Latin American independence; it had to make a decision regarding where its support would lie. If the Church continued to support the Spanish and Portuguese claims of empire in the Western Hemisphere then it ran the risk of losing support from the people of Latin America who had fought and died to win their freedom from those Iberian countries. But if the Church supported the Latin Americans in their struggle for independence, it would be able to continue to have a religious influence in the Western Hemisphere that extended into the political and social realms, but at the risk of upsetting Spain and Portugal by not supporting their claims in the New World.

In the end, the Church recognized the new countries of Latin America as legitimate entities, and proceeded to send bishops and cardinals throughout Latin America to strengthen its position in the hemisphere. But the countries of Latin America, having just fought for political and economic freedom, were uneasy about the continued authority of the Church and its European ties. This tension occasionally led to violence as Latin American governments attempted to distance themselves from the influence of the Church in economic and political matters. As a result, a general trend of secularism swept through the entire region, often accompanied by pessimism and occasional violence.

One example of this sort of conflict came in the late 1920s in Mexico. The Cristero Revolt erupted between the Church and the Mexican state and lasted from 1926 to 1929. The Cristeros (literally the army of *Cristo el Rey*, or Christ the King) believed that they were warriors of Christ and fought for religious inclusion and influence in the Mexican government. On the other side of the conflict was the federal government of Mexico, which was one of the Latin American bastions of positivism and progressivism, both ideologies that extolled the virtues of secularism and a reduced role for religion in state affairs.

In the summer of 1926, the Mexican government, under the leadership of President Plutarco Elías Calles, passed legislation designed to limit the power of the Church in public matters. Monasteries were outlawed, the Church was forbidden from owning property, and clergy could not wear the vestments of their office in public. By the autumn of 1926, several hundred Catholic freedom fighters decided these government acts were intolerable and reacted with violence against federal troops. Soon other acts of terrorism and violence followed, such as train bombings, bank robberies, arson, and murders. Eventually the Church and the Mexican government agreed upon a truce and some of the restrictions on the Church were lifted. But in other places in Latin America, revolutionaries fighting in the name of the Church continued to spread violence in places such as El Salvador, Colombia, and Chile.

Conclusions

Religion has been a driving force in the history of Latin America. From colonial times when the first priests arrived with Columbus and others, to independence when the Catholic Church sided with the revolutionaries in their struggle against Spain and Portugal, to the modern era when religion and politics clashed in multiple locations, religion has had a profound effect on the lives of the peoples of Latin America. Religion was used to indoctrinate Native Americans and African slaves alike. Religion was used as a political tool to influence the leadership of the colonies. Religion was the driving force behind extraordinary efforts by the clergy to convert non-Christians and save their souls. And religion has been responsible for both divisiveness and unification throughout Latin America as it influences at the same time tolerance and prejudice, charity and parsimony, violence and love.

Filmography

Films that depict religious themes in Latin American history are somewhat sparse. Three films will be reviewed below: *Yo, la Peor de Todas* (*I, the Worst of All*, 1990), *The Bridge of San Luis Rey* (2004), and *End of the Spear* (2005). *Yo, la Peor de Todas* portrays the seventeenth-century author and poet Sor Juana Inés de la Cruz in Mexico. Sor Juana is arguably the most gifted and celebrated writer of the colonial period in Mexican and Latin American history. *The Bridge of San Luis Rey* is a retelling of the bestselling book of the same name by Thornton Wilder. Published in 1927, Wilder's book earned him a Pulitzer Prize in 1928. Finally, *End of the Spear* is a recreation of actual events in Ecuador involving Christian missionaries and the fierce Waodani tribe, and their interactions that led to tragedy and ultimately forgiveness. Additionally, another film reviewed in chapter six of this book—*La Última Cena* (1976)—also deals with religion in a roundabout way. While this film has been included in the discussion of slavery in Latin America, it can also be viewed in the context of its religious undertones.

Yo, la Peor de Todas *(1990)*

Yo, la Peor de Todas was released in Argentina in 1990. Known in English as *I, the Worst of All*, the film opens in Mexico during the middle of the seventeenth century. Sor Juana Inés de la Cruz is a sister among other nuns in a convent. Almost immediately the film develops the relationship between Sor Juana and the viceroy of Mexico, Antonio Sebastían de Toledo, and even more importantly, his wife Leonor Carreto (although for the sake of simplicity in the film, these two individuals seem to be a combination of at least two different viceroys of Mexico and their wives). They become her patrons and sponsors, and many of her plays and other writings are dedicated to them.

Juana was something of an oddity in the convent. She had a personal library of more than 4000 books, plus scientific and musical instruments, among other interesting items. She spent most of her time in the convent reading, writing, and making observations with her objects of inquiry. This apparently non-ecclesiastical activity brought Juana to the attention of the archbishop of Mexico, Francisco de Aguiar y Seijas. He and other church officials were vexed with what they saw as laxity in the convent, and they desired to bring the nuns back in line. This included getting Juana to give up her more scholarly activities in exchange for more pious behavior. She refused to give up her passion for science, and the archbishop could not punish her because of the patronage of the viceroy.

After the tenure of Toledo expires, he is replaced as viceroy by the Marquis de la Laguna, whose wife, the vicereina María Luisa, became a close friend and confidant of Juana's. Eventually, Juana begins having frequent meetings with María Luisa and a close friendship begins. Juana writes poetry to María Luisa, who is named Phyllis and/or Lysis in the poems. These poems are full of passion, romance, and include very little religion. Some of the poems are eventually brought to the attention of the archbishop. He labels them scandalous for their sensual nature and orders Juana's rooms at the convent sealed shut. However, the viceroy intervenes, and by virtue of his position of authority over the archbishop, he orders her rooms reopened, and that she be permitted to carry on with her writing. At this point, the film develops more closely the close bond between María Luisa and Sor Juana that some have speculated may have become erotic in nature.

By 1688, Laguna and his wife are replaced and return to Spain. Now that Juana no longer has the protection and patronage of the viceroy, the archbishop Aguiar y Seijas begins to censure her. In 1690, Juana wrote a critique and evaluation of a sermon written several years earlier by a Portuguese priest named António de Vieira (who is quoted at the beginning of this chapter). Her argument was published under a pseudonym, but the archbishop and other clergymen knew that Juana was the author. She was again censured by the Church, which led to her publishing a retaliatory essay some months later defending the rights of women to study, write, and receive an education.

But with increasing pressure from the Church on Juana and members of her convent, by 1693 she finally renounced her "worldly" ways, agreed to give up her books, instruments, and other items, and confess her sins humbly in writing. It is interesting that while all of this controversy is occurring in Mexico, the former vicereina María Luisa publishes many of Juana's works in Spain, bringing much fame and attention to her and her writings.

The film concludes in 1695 with Juana helping her sick and dying sisters who are afflicted with a terrible plague. She has renounced her writings and

FIGURE 8.1 *Yo, la Peor de Todas* (*I, the Worst of All*, 1990, Juan Carlos Macías).

has spent the previous two years repenting and serving in the convent in a more ecclesiastical manner. But as a result of the plague and her exposure to it while treating her fellow sisters, Juana becomes ill and dies in June 1695.

This film is the only attempt to bring the life and career of Sor Juana to the big screen. Historically, much is known about her from her writings and the writings of others, and this film does a fairly accurate portrayal of her life in the convent. The film is based on a book by famed Latin American author Octavio Paz titled *Sor Juana: Or, the Traps of Faith*, written in 1988. The film is somewhat difficult to view; it appears to have been set as a play on a stage, and then filmed in that setting. As a result, the scenes are exceptionally dark in places and the dialogue is often quiet and difficult to hear. In addition, the film attempts to make the relationship between Juana and María Luisa more sensual and lesbian than it likely was. In fact, the description of the film on the jacket of the DVD proclaims "Lesbian passion seething behind convent walls. . . " This apparent expose on the erotic nature of Juana's relationship with María Luisa is perhaps overdone in the film's description, and does not reflect the friendship between the two women either in the film or in life. There is no doubt that the two women were close friends, but evidence for a closer relationship is somewhat lacking and seems to be implied. Their relationship may have been closer than what was considered appropriate for seventeenth-century Mexico, but evidence for a sexual relationship between the two women seems to be contrived and interpreted based on the content of some of Juana's poetry.

Ultimately, the value of the film is its depiction of the place of religion in Latin American politics during the colonial period. In the Spanish Empire in the New World, the Church and the state were often combined in overlapping jurisdictions. Indeed, some of the powerful viceroys of Mexico were clergymen. But the film also develops the occasional conflicts of interest between the Church and the state, and uses the history of Sor Juana as the backdrop on which to explore this topic.

The Bridge of San Luis Rey *(2004)*

In *The Bridge of San Luis Rey*, a novel by Thornton Wilder published in 1927, the story is divided between five fictional individuals who all fall to their deaths when an ancient Peruvian bridge collapses. The film of the same name weaves these storylines together and portrays the connections between these five people and the others that they interacted with. In the book and the film, the story is told via the testimony of a priest, Brother Juniper. Juniper, hearing of the catastrophe and the deaths of the five individuals, spends six years studying their lives in an attempt to determine if their deaths were the result of their sins and hence a punishment; or if their deaths were a reward for their good deeds in life, thus proffering them an end of mortal life and a return to God. Ultimately, the Inquisition, under the direction of the archbishop of Peru (played by Robert De Niro), puts Juniper on trial for heresy, for attempting to interpret the will of God in the same way one would go about making scientific observations during the Scientific Revolution and Enlightenment.

First of the five victims is the countess of Montemayor, a woman of monetary substance in Lima, but also known for her eccentricities, obesity, and drunkenness. When she is rebuffed by her daughter, who moves to Spain and will have nothing to do with her mother, the countess accepts a young woman from a local convent named Pepita to be her live-in companion. Pepita (who also becomes a victim of the bridge collapse) provides company and conversation for the older woman, who seems to be unable to enjoy the company of other socialites in Lima.

The next victim of the bridge collapse is a young man named Esteban. He has a twin brother Manuel and the two are so close to each other that they have developed a secret language that only the two of them know. They don't speak with other people, but they do work as scribes and letter writers for locals while they live in a Lima convent, the same convent where Pepita is from. Unbeknown to his brother, Manuel falls in love with a local actress named La Perichole. When Esteban finds out, Manuel feels guilty and swears never to see her again.

Uncle Pio is the fourth victim. He is La Perichole's advisor and professional agent. He arranges her performances, and even organizes a specific event for the viceroy of Peru. On the night of the event, the countess of Montemayor attends the concert hall. She is obviously drunk and becomes a distraction to the whole theater. On stage, La Perichole becomes annoyed and begins to mock the countess by imitating her on stage. She pokes fun of the countess' obesity, her drunkenness, and her general lack of social graces. The audience is amused, but the viceroy later orders La Perichole to offer a formal apology to the countess for her behavior in the theater. Here the film develops the fact that the Church is enmeshed in all the different activities of the city. The clergy approve the theater pieces, assign individuals to specific occupations, and control many other secular matters as well. Furthermore, Manuel, Esteban, and Pepita are all associated with a local convent, continuing the development of the Church's role in Lima society.

One evening La Perichole calls for Manuel to draft a letter for her. He refuses to write for her anymore. As a result, he and Esteban decide that they will no longer write for anyone, and they take a job unloading ships on the docks. In a freak accident, Manuel injures his leg on a piece of sharp metal. Esteban attempts to care for his brother by tending to the wound, but as time goes on the gash becomes infected. In increasing pain, Manuel and Esteban grow further apart until the infection grows too great and Manuel dies. Esteban is so distraught by the death of his twin that he attempts to commit suicide but is stopped by a ship captain named Alvarado who not only saves Esteban from death, but also convinces him to sail with him on the captain's ship, an opportunity that will take him out of Lima and away from his former life.

Meanwhile, the countess of Montemayor discovers that her daughter in Spain is going to have a child. She is not welcome to visit her daughter there because of the tense relationship between them, so she decides to go on a pilgrimage to a nearby shrine where she will petition for the healthy delivery of her grandchild. Pepita goes along with her to be a companion and to help when needed.

La Perichole believes that her career is over because she contracts smallpox and her face is disfigured and scarred with pock marks. So, she retires to an estate in the country. Also while at the estate, La Perichole has a child, who she names Don Jaime (the fifth victim of the bridge's collapse). When Uncle Pio visits her, she is ashamed of her scarred complexion and refuses to see him. He implores her to allow him to take her son Jaime so that he can get an education and learn a trade. She ultimately concedes and the young boy becomes Uncle Pio's companion.

All of these separate storylines have proceeded simultaneously, and all have been somewhat connected. But at this juncture of the film, all of the storylines connect directly as the countess of Montemayor, Pepita, Uncle Pio, Don Jaime, and Esteban all attempt to cross the old bridge at the same time. When the bridge collapses, all five fall to their deaths. The thing that all five had in common was La Perichole. She represented something to each of the five, whether through love (as is the case with Esteban), familial relationship (as with Uncle Pio and Don Jaime), or ridicule (as with the countess and Pepita).

After their deaths, the film returns to the trial of Brother Juniper. He has spent six years doing research, conducting interviews, and attempting intricate mathematical equations, all in an attempt to understand why these five particular people were killed on that day at that exact time. During Juniper's trial, La Perichole comes to testify in defense of Brother Juniper. But the viceroy refuses to hear her testimony, stating that this woman is not La Perichole; he doesn't recognize her because of the damage done to her face by smallpox. In the end, Juniper is condemned for heresy and is burned at the stake in the town square along with the book he has written outlining all of his conclusions about their deaths.

The Bridge of San Luis Rey portrays colonial Peru as a society that is under the influence of both the Crown and the Church. The fact that both the viceroy and the archbishop sit in trial on Brother Juniper demonstrates the coexistence of the secular and ecclesiastical. The film also depicts the role of the Church in stamping out heresy in all forms and at all levels, including among the clergy. And even for those individuals in society who were less religiously inclined, the Church still played a role in their everyday lives. Indeed, none of the five individuals who fell from the bridge that day were that religious in nature. But their deaths sparked the research of a clergyman and eventually led to his death for trying to interpret what their deaths might mean to God.

End of the Spear *(2005)*

The final film for this chapter is *End of the Spear*, directed by Jim Hanon. This docudrama tells the story of Nathan Saint and his companions as they try to convert the Waodani Indians of Ecuador to Christianity in the 1950s. The film is based on a true story, although some of the details in the film were modified to fit with the film medium, or to present the details in a more dramatic way. The principle Waodani personality is Mincayani, a fierce warrior who does not trust the coming of these Christian missionaries.

Nathan Saint is one of a handful of missionaries—men and women—who have come to Ecuador to preach to the Waodani, a reclusive and aggressive tribe of native Amazonians. They are known for their quickness to fight, even among themselves. Saint flies over the jungle area in a yellow airplane and soon discovers where the Waodani are living. Now long after spotting the tribe from the air, Saint and the other missionaries land on a sandbar in the middle of a river near their settlement. This area will be used in the future as a place to use as a basecamp for the missionaries as they approach the Waodani village. As Saint prepares to leave for a subsequent visit to the tribe, his son Stevie asks him if he will shoot the Waodani if they try to harm him. Saint replies that he cannot shoot them because they are not ready for Heaven. The film shows that the missionaries are determined to convert the Waodani regardless of what the consequences—economic, social, or political—may be on the tribe in the long run.

Eventually the missionaries begin to interact with the Waodani from the sandbar. The missionaries speak a few phrases in Waodani but not enough to really communicate the gospel to them. The Waodani are afraid of the foreigners, claiming that they are cannibals. Through a series of misunderstandings, the Waodani become angry and begin to kill the missionaries with spears. As Nathan Saint lies dying from his spear wounds, he says to Mincayani in Waodani that he is his friend. Then, when the missionaries are dead, the Indians begin to attack the airplane, tearing it apart and leaving it to rust.

When other foreigners arrive at the sandbar looking for the missionaries, the Waodani decide to move further into the jungle to get away from the incursions of the missionaries. Meanwhile, Stevie mourns the loss of his father and reads accounts of the missionaries in magazines and watches them on home movies. The wives of the slain missionaries continue to visit the jungle to contact the Waodani. These women have befriended a Waodani woman named Dayumae who was captured by foreigners when she was a child. Now a converted Christian, she is able to translate for the two groups.

Through a series of meetings with the Waodani, Dayumae explains that they need to stop killing and do the will of Waengongi, the Waodani word for God. She explains to Mincayani and the others that Waengongi had a son who was speared so that the people could live in peace and not harm each other any longer.

As time moves on, some of the Waodani begin to accept Christianity and change their behavior. Warriors refuse to kill any longer and the people begin to build a church in the jungle. But soon a group of Indians who are enemies of the Waodani, called the Aenomenani, come to attack. The Waodani are split about what they should do; should they attack the Aenomenani, or attempt to appease them? Ultimately, the Aenomenani decide not to attack the peaceful Waodani, and it is quickly discovered that the Aenomenani have contracted polio and are dying.

Eventually, Stevie and his mother leave Ecuador and move back to the United States, leaving behind Stevie's Aunt Rachel, who wishes to stay with the Waodani and continue to teach them. Years later, after Rachel's death, Stevie (now just Steve) and his wife return to Ecuador for Rachel's burial. Steve discovers that the Waodani are more Westernized now, and have for the most part accepted Christianity. Mincayani decides to take Steve to the location where his father Nathan Saint died. When they get there, Mincayani tells Steve that he was the one who killed his father. Mincayani then wants Steve to kill him in retribution. When Steve refuses, the two are reconciled to each other and eventually become friends. Finally, in 1995, Steve and his family return again to Ecuador to live permanently with the Waodani.

End of the Spear is an interesting film that shows the evangelization among Native Indian groups in Latin America. The film portrays the changes that come about over time among the tribe, and how their lifestyle evolved as a result of their acceptance of Christianity. It also showed the increased incursion of Westernization into the area as a result of continued contact. However, some of the religious elements of the story are glossed over in the film so that the story of the missionaries and their more personal interactions with the Waodani can be developed.

The film's reception in 2005 was marred by the revelation that the actor who played both Nathan and Steve Saint, Chad Allen, is openly gay. Many Christian groups boycotted the film because they did not believe that a religiously based film should have a gay man in the leading role. Unfortunately, this controversy overshadowed the message of the movie, and the film became somewhat marginalized because of the criticism of some Evangelical Christian groups that encouraged people not to see the film.

But aside from the homophobic reaction of some groups in the United States, *End of the Spear* remains an important piece of film literature on the nature of Christianization in Latin America, and the progress that Protestant Evangelical groups have made in a region of Latin America where Catholicism has been the predominant religion for hundreds of years. During the early years of the twentieth century, protestant groups increasingly traveled to many different countries in Latin America, bringing their version of Christianity to the native groups and city populations. And while the film tends to mute the overall result of these types of conversion in Latin American communities, it remains a good tool for showing the continuing work of Christian groups in Latin America.

Further Reading

Gonzalez, Justo L., and Ondina E. Gonzalez. *Christianity in Latin America.* Cambridge: Cambridge University Press, 2007.

Hitt, Russell. *Jungle Pilot: The Gripping Story of the Life and Witness of Nate Saint, Martyred Missionary to Ecuador.* Grand Rapids, MI: Discovery House Publishers, 1997.

Lynch, John. *New Worlds: A Religious History of Latin America.* New Haven, CT: Yale University Press, 2012.

Maurer, Eugenio, et al. *The Indian Face of God in Latin America.* Maryknoll, NY: Orbis Books, 1996.

Paz, Octavio. *Sor Juana: Or, the Traps of Faith.* New York: Belknap Press, 1988.

Penyak, Lee M. and Walter J. Petry. *Religion in Latin America.* Maryknoll, NY: Orbis Books, 2006.

Schwaller, John Frederick. *The History of the Catholic Church in Latin America.* New York: New York University Press, 2011.

Wilder, Thornton. *The Bridge of San Luis Rey.* New York: Perennial Classics, 1999.

9

WOMEN IN LATIN AMERICA

The nation's government has just handed me the bill that grants us our civil rights.
I am receiving it before you, certain that I am accepting this on behalf of all Argentinean women, and I can feel my hands tremble with joy as they grasp the laurel
proclaiming victory.

Eva Perón

Introduction

For many years, historians did not pay much attention to women in Latin
American history and, in some cases, argued that there were no women in
Latin American history! The little information on women's roles focused
mainly on family situations where women were mostly under the control of
men. They lived in a male-dominated society and many historians believed
that women were virtually anonymous in the historical record. For example,
in legal documents, a woman's name would only appear on baptism and marriage certificates, and that's pretty much it. Women who were involved in
court cases were usually represented by their husbands and their names rarely
appeared in the court records unless they were women of nobility, substance,
and wealth.

However, in the last half-century or so, historians have repeatedly gone back
to these old documents in search of women's experiences, and they have found
more than they expected. Historians in the nineteenth and early twentieth centuries did not find women in the colonial documents because that was not what
they were looking for.

Women in Colonial Latin America

Between 1500 and 1825, women played an important role in Latin America in terms of family life, and as the guarantors of honor and rectitude in Latin American society. And, in Latin American society in the colonial years, women found themselves divided into two categories: *mujer de razón* (woman of reason), and *mujer sin razón* (women without reason).

Mujer de Razón

Mujer de razón primarily referred to white women from Spain or Portugal, or white women of Iberian background who were born in the colonies. These white women could be women of substance and wealth, or women married to merchants, laborers, and other men who played an essential role in society. Wealthy and high-status women in the colonies lived lives of luxury, frequently married to wealthy landowners and men involved in the politics of the colonies. Women's place in society was to maintain the social status of elite families, or to preserve the pride and honor of middle-class families who didn't have significant wealth, but did work hard to keep society moving along. During the early years of the colonial period, women were significantly outnumbered by men in the colonies, sometimes by as much as three-to-one.

In colonial Latin America, Iberian women remained a small percentage of the population for many years. In the 1520s only around 15 percent of immigrants to the New World were women, and that number never went higher than roughly 30 percent by the turn of the seventeenth century. The women who did come to the Americas were often wives of prominent landowners, merchants, traders, or wholesalers in the colonies. Some women came across the Atlantic listed as "servants" on official ship's logs, which was probably a polite way of saying they were courtesans for the wealthy, or prostitutes that sold their services to middle-class men. The role of wealthy and high-class women in colonial society was to transmit domestic material culture and religious social values to their children so that those offspring could become productive, honorable Spanish and Portuguese citizens later in life.

Under Iberian law and tradition, a woman lived under her father's authority until she married, and then she transferred to her husband's authority. This was to protect women from abuse and from their own frailties. Upper-class women were secluded from society when young and even until the age of courtship, and were the bastion of the family's honor. A woman was supposed to protect her honor and that of her family at all costs. A woman's chastity, virtue, and fidelity were all reflections of the honor of the entire family. If a woman's honor failed or was compromised, the honor of the entire family could be tarnished.

Women were obligated to preserve and safeguard their virginity at all costs. Men were free to visit prostitutes and have extramarital affairs. This resulted in a moral double standard. If a man engaged in sexually explicit behavior, the family's honor was not tarnished in the same way it would have been if a daughter or sister were involved in the same behavior. Men were not held to the same moral standards as women, and illegitimate children (born out of wedlock) were relegated to the status of second-class citizens in much of the Spanish and Portuguese empires.

Wealthy women were generally found within the confines of their own homes and estates. They ran households but rarely entered into public except for social situations such as attending the theater, taking part in religious services, purchasing items, and attending or participating in official ceremonies such as weddings, baptisms, funerals, and so on. It was common for women of reason to marry men much older than they were, and it was not exceptional for young women to marry men who were widowers. Marriages were frequently arranged by fathers or other male family representatives.

All but the wealthiest women in society were likely illiterate. But women from high society would be trained in the ideals of proper behavior including reading, writing, music, embroidery, and other sophisticated activities. Young women were generally separated from young men in childhood and did not interact much with non-familial males until chaperoned courtship. Divorce was very rare and women could not seek a divorce except under extraordinary circumstances. Scandalous adultery, long-term physical abuse, abandonment, and bigamy were all potentially grounds for divorce for upper-class women.

Some women from high or low society found it desirable to enter nunneries or convents. These locations were run by women and were separated from the outside world. Occasionally women would choose this lifestyle in order to have more control over their own decisions and destinies. In other situations, women entered into cloistered life to avoid suitors or to escape persecution for poor moral decisions or dishonorable actions. One such woman who entered a convent in order to free herself from the strictures of society placed on women was Sor Juana Inés de la Cruz (see Chapter 8), who was one of the most important female intellects of colonial Latin America. During the seventeenth century she wrote extensively, producing plays, stories, poetry, songs, and textbooks. She also painted, played musical instruments, studied science, and engaged in a host of other activities that would not have been available to her had she not secluded herself from society within the walls of the convent. She eventually lost all of her books and musical instruments in order to meet the pious demands of the convent, but she remained a writer until her death.

Mujer sin Razón

On the other side of the coin was the *mujer sin razón* or the "woman without reason." Women in this category were not documented as extensively as women of reason, and therefore less is known of their lives, activities, and lifestyles. Suffice it to say that women without reason were all the things that women of reason were not. Women in this category were usually poor and often from racially mixed backgrounds—Indian, Mestizo, African, and Mulatto women all fell into this category. Poor white women were also considered women without reason, but their status was not considered as wretched as women of mixed racial heritage.

But even though the lives of these women were not as privileged as those of the *mujer de razón*, they did enjoy some privileges in society that elite women did not. For example, poor and racially mixed women could be more economically independent, because they were permitted and even encouraged to work outside the home. They labored in a variety of occupations that brought income to poor families, and this also made these women more visible public figures than elusive wealthy white women. These occupations included making pottery, sewing, weaving, food and drink production (including alcoholic beverages), running bakeries and small markets where products would be purchased such as cloth, candles, candy, cigars and other tobacco products, household items, and other things.

Women without reason were also not held to the same strict standards of morality as wealthy elite women. Interestingly, if a lower-class woman did not want to follow the mandate of her family in an arranged marriage, she might get pregnant with the child of a man she desired so that the arranged marriage would have to be cancelled in lieu of a marriage to the father of the child. In this way, the *mujer sin razón* could be seen to have had more sexual freedom than wealthier women whose sexuality was constantly guarded and sheltered.

Finally, non-elite white women in colonial society and in modern Latin American cities and villages were often employed as domestic servants, washerwomen, and were engaged in childcare for the wealthy. Women of mixed racial heritage could also be employed by wealthier families for more menial household work such as cleaning, cooking, making soap and candles, and working outside the home in gardens, courtyards, and sometimes in fields of grain or sugarcane.

In all, *mujer sin razón* are not represented in colonial documents as prominently as *mujer de razón*, but in actuality, they were the backbone of colonial Spanish and Portuguese society; they quietly kept the social order moving forward and were the unsung foundational heroes on which colonial society rested. Without the *mujer sin razón*, colonial society would not have proceeded and would have been very difficult because they played such a prominent—if invisible—role in Latin American colonial lives.

Women in Modern Latin America

After 1825, conditions for women in Latin America changed very little. The same societal norms and customs prevailed, and life still centered on the home, marriage, religion, polite society, and children. The division between white women and women of color was still vast, and the ideals of women's honor and chastity continued. But during the revolutions that brought an end to colonialism in Latin America, women began to assume new roles in society that had not been possible for them earlier. During the revolutionary wars, women served as couriers, informants, and occasionally as spies. They also worked in field hospitals caring for the sick and wounded. They traveled with soldiers and armies where they served in a variety of ways that ranged from cooking to prostitution. And although it was rare, there are some documents that indicate that a few women fought with Simón Bolívar's forces in Venezuela in the early years of the nineteenth century.

After independence, during the early national period, women were expected to return to their traditional roles, even though they had demonstrated their abilities in politics, organizations and economics, and even revolutionary activism. But women were still not permitted to hold public office, vote, or serve as witnesses in courts, and they were still considered the guardians of familial honor. One gain was in education. Women's opportunities were still not equal to men's, but if they had the money to attend school, they did have more options in terms of available curriculum than before.

During the early years of the twentieth century, rural women continued to work as seamstresses, artisans, and food preparers, but wealthier women began to move into new occupations, employed as factory workers, clerks, nurses, and teachers. Early feminist ideas began to trickle into Latin America during these years, and Latin American women felt the desire for equal rights in voting and education, not to mention wages and job opportunities. However, there were some women who resisted these changes as well. Some believed that these new rights would erode family and home life and promote promiscuity and other problems. Nevertheless, Latin American women became to exercise more freedom as they traveled abroad more frequently and returned home with ideas about fashion, education, and feminism that caught on quickly. National women's suffrage became a reality in the United States in 1920. In Latin American countries, these rights quickly followed. In the 1930s, Ecuador, Brazil, Uruguay, Cuba, and El Salvador all granted women the right to vote and participate in politics. During the years between 1940 and 1960, the rest of Latin American nations adopted women's suffrage as national policy, and this paved the way for women to enter into politics at the local and national levels.

In the realm of education, but the mid-twentieth century, the majority of teachers in Latin American public and private schools were women. And although the literacy rate was generally about the same for poor women as during previous centuries, literacy among wealthier, educated women began to rise precipitously. Still, rural women continued to work in traditional labor roles—planting, harvesting, tending animals, and sales at local markets made up a significant percentage of female labor in most Latin American countries.

Nevertheless, more and more women began to enter into politics. This was difficult in some Latin American countries ruled by military dictators. However, during the last two decades of the twentieth century, women were likely to be promoted to cabinet positions in the regimes of some Central and South American governments, although these cabinet positions still reflected the traditional roles of women, such as secretary of health and secretary of education. Women have also been elected to prominent political positions in several Latin American governments, some serving as heads of state, surpassing in some ways the glass ceiling that remained in the United States into the twenty-first century. Since the 1990s, several women have served as heads of state in their respective countries: Lidia Gueiler as interim president in Bolivia; Violeta Chamorro as president of Nicaragua; Eugenia Charles served as the prime minister in the Dominican Republic; Ertha Pascal-Trouillot as president of Haiti; Rosalía Arteaga Serrano was the president of Ecuador; Michelle Bachelet of Chile; Dilma Vana Roussef of Brazil; Cristina Fernández de Kirchner of Argentina; and Mireya Elisa Moscoso was the president of Panama. All of these women served their presidencies in the 1990s, with a few exceptions in the 1980s and late 1970s. This political reality is significant when one considers that in the United States, no woman has served in a governmental office higher than secretary of state.

Conclusions

Throughout the history of Latin America women have played and continue to play an important role. It is regrettable that history ignored women in the history of Latin America for so many years, and now that women are being offered their proper place in the history of the region, this history is becoming richer and more complete. And while Latin American countries often are stereotyped in terms of *machismo*, or male-dominated society that depreciates the roles of women, in actual fact, Latin American countries have surpassed other countries in the Western Hemisphere (including the United States) and Europe in permitting women roles in public society, politics, economics, and other areas. In addition, throughout much of Latin America's history, where women have born the load of domestic responsibility of household and children, they have shaped the leaders of Latin American countries who have, in turn, given place for feminist advocates in Latin American societies.

Filmography

Filmmakers have often depicted the conditions and aspirations of women in Latin American countries in films that may or may not be specifically designed to highlight women's influences. Some of these films come from original pieces of literature such as *Like Water for Chocolate* (1992). Others, such as *Camila* (1984), the story of Camila O'Gorman, a member of Argentina's upper-class society in the 1800s who runs away with a priest, Father Ladislao Gutiérrez, are biopic pieces that describe the lives of important women and their contributions to the societies in which they lived.

In this chapter, three films are analyzed, *Eva Perón: The True Story* (1996), *Frida* (2002), and *María Full of Grace* (2004). Each of these films depicts various struggles and challenges that Latin American woman are forced to surmount in a predominantly patriarchal society. *Eva Perón* and *Frida* are biographical renditions of the lives of Eva Perón, the wife of Argentine president and political leader Juan Domingo Perón, and Frida Kahlo, a Mexican painter, activist, and wife of Diego Rivera, another famous Mexican painter. *María Full of Grace*, set in modern Colombia, is a fictional film (although promotional materials for the film proclaimed that it was based on 1000 true stories) that portrays the difficulties many Latin American women face because of the forces of marginalization and abuse that they endure. All three films are epic in their scope and design, and all illustrate the concept of the feminine place in Latin American society in the twentieth and twenty-first centuries.

Eva Perón: The True Story *(1996)*

The film *Eva Perón: The True Story* (1996) is Argentina's answer to the American film *Evita* (1996) staring Madonna and Antonio Banderas. Argentina was so appalled that the American musical production would star Madonna as their beloved Eva, that they commissioned their own film to portray the significant events in the life of Eva Perón, her husband Juan Domingo Perón, the president of Argentina Juan Domingo Perón who ruled Argentina between 1946 and 1955, and her importance to Argentineans.

Following a brief exploration of the differences between Eva and her husband Juan, wherein the viewer is informed that by 1951, she wanted to be the vice-president of Argentina and Juan is not so sure he wants the same thing, the film proceeds with the narrative of her life, beginning with the funeral scene of her father when she was only seven years old. Eva was his illegitimate daughter by one of his mistresses, and she, along with her other siblings and their mother, attempted to enter the place where their father's body was on display preceding his burial. After initially being denied entrance, they were permitted a brief viewing and then quickly escorted off the property. Eva's feelings of insecurity and illegitimacy would beleaguer her for the rest of her life, convincing her that she always had something to prove to others.

Later, the film develops the differences between Eva and her husband Juan. She is charismatic and uses her personality to defuse a union worker's strike. She strengthens her husband's position and convinces the workers to return to their jobs. On the other hand, her husband is somewhat closed and private, preferring to let others appear in the spotlight while he runs things behind the scenes. Eva Perón soon becomes the representative of the people of Argentina, while her husband is portrayed as an advocate for the establishment and the Argentinean military. Soon, crates of goods, food, and supplies that are labeled as resources from the Eva Perón Foundation begin to travel throughout the country to assist the poor and needy. Eva creates relief organizations for the poor and uses her position as one of the people who rose from humble beginnings to the top to build her reputation and that of her husband.

Juan Domingo Perón's political ideology, known as *Peronismo* (a moderate ideology that was considered less aggressive or extreme as communism on the left and capitalism on the right) is not really developed in the film, but Eva does question Juan regarding whether *Peronismo* is a vehicle for dictatorship or popular revolution. The film develops Eva's conflicting desires for increasing independence from her husband's long political shadow on the one hand, while at the same time her need to stand with him in the highest positions of political power in the Argentine government on the other. But her husband's political opponents begin to talk of orchestrating a coup to remove him from power, prompting Eva to work even harder to proclaim the benefits of living under *Peronismo* in Argentina.

Eva often laments her illegitimate status, and being pulled down by those who are jealous of her success, while at the same time rising above the standing of her detractors. In this vein she asks her husband Juan if he will support her in her bid for the vice-presidency of the country. He is very noncommittal and repeatedly changes the subject, indicating his uneasiness about her growing popularity and status as a representative of the poor.

But as her reputation among the people continues to grow, she is also confronted by Argentinean women of high social rank who are in charge of the Women's Charity Association. They inform her that because of her illegitimate status, and her previous occupation as a second-rate actress, a profession that many considered demeaning, she would not be permitted to occupy the position of president of the society, even though the president's wife had always held that position in the past. She rises to the occasion and effectively dissolves their organization, stating that it is now redundant because she has created the Eva Perón Foundation to take its place. The women are rudely dismissed and once again Eva is reminded of her illegitimacy and reduced status in Argentinean high society.

As the film progresses, more attention to the fact that Eva Perón, while still relatively young and at the height of her influence, is—unknown to everyone but her doctors and husband—suffering from terminal cancer. She unknowingly laments that her body is somehow betraying her and taking away her ability to work among the people that adore her. Her husband Juan continues much as before, unconcerned about talk of a coup and hiding the fact that Eva has cancer from her.

Then, the critical moment arrives. A huge assembly, resembling a mob of people, amasses outside the presidential palace in Buenos Aires. Juan Perón speaks to the crowd and tries to assuage their concerns about his leadership and apparent inability to aid them in their poverty. The people cry for Eva to come to the balcony and accept their nomination for vice-president of Argentina. She is eventually brought to the balcony and instructed to calm the crowd. Interestingly, the film footage that portrays the large crowd of more than two million people appears to be actual footage from the time that the riot took place in Argentina in 1951. These incorporated images lend the film a striking reality, especially concerning the charisma Eva had, and the fascination the people of Argentina held for her. She pleads with Juan to allow her to accept the people's wishes and be nominated as Argentina's vice-president. He tells her outright that she cannot accept their wishes. He then tells her to use her influence to disperse the crowd. However, the people will not leave. Unrelenting, Juan tells her to accede to the people's wishes without actually agreeing to give her the nomination. When Eva tells the mob that she will do what they want, the cheer and the trouble is averted.

Finally, Juan Perón comes clean with Eva and tells her frankly that there are two reasons she cannot be Argentina's vice-president. First, the military opposes her for the position of vice-president. And more importantly, she cannot hold the office because she has cancer. For the rest of the film Eva is depicted trying to continue her charitable work from her bed. But her condition worsens and she eventually dies at the young age of 33.

The popularity of Eva Perón in Argentina's history cannot be overstated. After her death, tens of thousands of people tried to see her body lying in state in Buenos Aires, some being wounded in the press of the people, and eight people who were actually crushed to death in the throng. And following her death, some compared Eva to the Virgin Mary as the second most important woman in Argentina, if not in the Western Hemisphere. During her career, she succeeded in gaining women the right to vote in Argentina, provided aid to countless millions of Argentineans suffering from poverty, and helped her husband maintain his paternalistic image as the leader of Argentina. Her birthday is still celebrated in Argentina to this day, and her image and representation will always be a part of Argentina's heritage.

Juan Carlos DeSanzo reviewed the film *Eva Perón* for the *New York Times*, and observed that "while there is enough drama in her story to serve as the basis for countless movies, this one is of particular interest because it is by her countrymen." And in the *Chicago Reader*, Lisa Alspector states:

> Without singing even once, Esther Goris blows Madonna away as Eva Perón . . . This slow-paced movie may appear dry and morbid compared to the musical version, but it's an effective character study with plenty of subtext . . . *Eva Perón* enables you to marvel at a character who's potent enough to command authority in a pink dress and frilly hat, and passionate enough to evince fervor when bedridden; you're compelled to ponder her complex motivations throughout.

Frida *(2002)*

The film *Frida* (2002), directed by Julie Taymor, presents the life of troubled Mexican painter Frida Kahlo (portrayed by Salma Hayek). As a child she is depicted as a girl willing to challenge authority and do what she wants. For example, she dresses as a boy for a family portrait, much to the vexation of her parents. But while she is still young, a bus she was riding in crashed and her body was pierced through with a rough piece of metal. In the accident she broke several bones and was forced to wear a body cast for months. Because she had nothing else to do while confined and healing, she began to paint.

When she is again able to walk, she seeks out the famous Mexican painter Diego Rivera, and asks him if her paintings are any good. He praises her work as original and brilliantly conceived, as something out of the norm and not reminiscent of other painters of the day. Eventually Kahlo and Rivera have an affair and, after his marriage falls apart, she becomes his new wife. Their marriage is illustrated throughout the film as a rather open situation. Both of them had multiple sexual partners throughout their marriage and lives, so their relationship seems to have been built on their mutual production of art, and their need for stability in their lives when both of them endured different traumatic events.

Eventually Rivera is commissioned to paint a mural in the lobby of Rockefeller Center in New York. They travel to the United States and Kahlo continues her own painting while her husband works on the mural. But when her mother dies, she returns to Mexico prematurely while Rivera remains in New York to finish the mural. Eventually, Rivera includes a portrait of Vladimir Lenin in the mural, sparking the ire of the commissioners of the painting. When Rivera refuses to remove the portrait, he is paid and the entire mural wall is destroyed and replaced, whereupon Rivera also returns to Mexico.

Kahlo continues to paint, mostly self-portraits. But when Rivera has an affair with her sister, she becomes increasingly depressed and the film demonstrates how her attitudes and sentiments are reflected in her paintings of that time period. However, she also has her own sexual affairs, but she and Rivera seem to continue their strange relationship with each other despite these various infidelities.

Around 1937, Leon Trotsky, one of Lenin's revolutionary leaders in the Russian Revolution that toppled the tsar of Russia and ushered in the communist government of the USSR, comes to Mexico seeking political asylum. Trotsky is attempting to escape the purges of Joseph Stalin in the Soviet Union that followed Lenin's death. Trotsky had received death threats in Russia and sought to distance himself as far from the USSR as possible. While in Mexico, Trotsky and his wife are briefly entertained by Rivera and Kahlo. The film shows the scene where Trotsky and Kahlo climb to the top of the Pyramid of the Sun at the ruins of Teotihuacán north of Mexico City. Soon after, Trotsky and Kahlo

FIGURE 9.1 Frida Khalo in *Frida* (2002, Miramax).

have an affair, and he and he and his wife soon move to a different location in Mexico where Trotsky is eventually assassinated by Soviet agents.

In 1939, Kahlo travels to Paris for an exhibition of her works. Director Julie Taymor here chooses to focus on Kahlo's bisexual relationships instead of the actual art exhibition. Taymor also portrays the various affairs that Rivera has while Kahlo is away, particularly her relationship with Josephine Baker. It is regrettable that Taymor chose to focus more on their sexuality instead of their work, which overshadows the importance of Kahlo's career and instead capitalizes on her personal infidelities. In the end, Kahlo's trip to Paris is very successful and the Louvre purchases some of her work for display.

At the end of the film, Kahlo discovers that her feet have gangrene, and they will need to be amputated. She is eventually confined to bed and told that she cannot attend a celebration in her honor at a newly opening exhibition of her works. So, true to her independent nature and character, she does what she wants instead of what her doctors tell her to do. She has herself transported to the exhibition while still in her bed.

Overall, the film *Frida* does a good job of describing the troubled life of Frida Kahlo, her tempestuous marriage to Diego Rivera, and her art. But the film could have focused more on her career as an artist and less on the scintillating aspects of her life. Director Taymor seems to have chosen to portray the sensational characteristics of Kahlo's life at the expense of her personal victories over opposition, and the development of her career as an artist. Nevertheless, Frida Kahlo's life was more than just her art, and the erotic aspects of her life certainly also had an effect on her art, just as did victory over tribulation and misfortune.

In 2002, Roger Ebert reviewed *Frida*. Toward the end of his writing, he notes that "Taymor obviously struggled with the material . . . Sometimes we feel as if the film careens from one colorful event to another without respite, but sometimes it must have seemed to Frida Kahlo as if her life did, too." Ultimately, the life of Frida Kahlo is summed up as a life "that ended at 46 and yet made longer lives seem underfurnished."

María Full of Grace (2004)

María Full of Grace (*María, llenna eres de gracia*, 2004) is a Columbian film that explores the drug trade in Latin America, and specifically the trafficking of cocaine from Colombia to the United States. The use of drug "mules," or human carriers of heroin and cocaine pellets, is the focus of the story, depicted through the life of a seventeen year old pregnant girl named María. María works in a flower-packaging farm, preparing rose blooms to be sold. She takes her earnings home to give to her family in order to take care of her younger siblings and nephews who are sick. She hates the fact that her family is poor, but she nevertheless quits her job when she is treated poorly at work.

Then she finds out that she is pregnant. Her boyfriend offers to marry her but after telling him she doesn't love him, she exercises her strong will and decides to move on without him. Eventually she meets a man who tells her that she can make a lot of money as a drug "mule". After talking with a few drug traffickers, she is deemed fit for the job and told that she will be sent to the United States for around a week. She will earn several million Columbian pesos (thousands of US dollars) for her work transporting the drugs. She also meets another "mule" named Lucy who helps prepare her for what is to come.

When the time comes for her to receive her cargo, she goes to the back room of a local pharmacy where she swallows more than 60 "pills" that are filled with heroin. These pills are constructed by cutting off the fingers from rubber gloves, filling them with drugs, and then sealing them in a way that they will not open while inside the stomach of the mule. She is then given some cash, a plane ticket, a passport and visa, and the address of a hotel in New York City. Finally, she is intimidated with threats of what will happen to her family if she doesn't do what he is supposed to do. In a harrowing scene aboard the airplane, María accidentally excretes one of the pellets in the aircraft's lavatory. She quickly cleans the pellet and swallows it again so that she will not lose the money she has been promised. When she lands in the United States, she is stopped by Customs and asked a lot of questions about the purpose of her visit. The Customs officials have suspicions that she is carrying drugs in her stomach and want to do an X-ray on her but when they discover that she is pregnant, they let her go. One of the other mules on the plane is arrested after an X-ray discovers the drugs in her stomach, and María's friend Lucy begins to get very ill.

María is eventually picked up by some men and taken to a hotel to wait for the pills to "pass." At the hotel, Lucy dies because one of the pills burst inside her, and the men who are watching the mules cut her open to get the drugs out of her stomach. María panics and tries to make a run for it. She takes the drugs that she has passed and goes to the New York City apartment where Lucy's sister lives. Lucy's sister lets her stay for a couple of days but when she discovers that María is a drug smuggler and that Lucy is now dead, she kicks María out. María eventually calls the men from the hotel who had been guarding the girls. They come, recover the drug pills, and pay her for her services. The film concludes with María making the decision to remain in New York instead of returning to her family in Colombia.

While this film explores the conditions of mules who help traffickers of drugs move their product across international borders, it is also a commentary of the role of women in some Latin American countries. Most drug mules are women and they often take on the work willingly in order to help pay bills or debts, and make ends meet for their families. Their exploitation takes advantage of their humble circumstances and the fact that they are dependent on men for their financial support. In the film, the resolution comes not when the drugs are delivered, or when Lucy dies, or when María is paid what is owed her: the climax comes in the last minutes of the film when María exerts her independence and decides to stay in the United States instead of becoming another victim of the drug traffic. Ultimately, for María it comes down to her decision to not be victimized, in her eyes, by the needs that her family place upon her. She has an opportunity to escape from her past, and she takes it.

New York Times film critic Stephen Holden reviewed *María Full of Grace* in 2003. After delivering a tense overview of the film, he observes:

> *María Full of Grace* sustains a documentary authenticity that is as astonishing as it is offhand. Even when you are on the edge of your seat, it never sacrifices a calm, clear-sighted humanity for the sake of melodrama or cheap moralizing . . . María's desperate decision may be reprehensible on one level. But on another, deeper level, it is an act of courageous self-assertion. You applaud every step of her scary lunge toward personal liberation.

In 2004, Roger Ebert also reviewed the film. He noticed that the film "is an extraordinary experience for many reasons, including, oddly, its willingness to be ordinary. We see everyday life here, plausible motives, convincing decisions, and characters who live at ground level." Ebert observes that just as María was bored and sick of her job preparing roses for sale at the beginning of the film, so are the thugs who guard the mules in the hotel just "as bored by their job as María was with the roses. Most drug movies are about glamorous stars surrounded by special effects. Meanwhile, in a world almost below the radar, the Marías and Lucys hopefully board their flights with stomachs full of death."

Further Reading

Fraser, Nicholas and Marysa Navarro. *Evita: The Real Lives of Eva Peron.* London: Andre Deutsch, 2003.

Fuentes, Carlos. *The Diary of Frida Kahlo: An Intimate Self-Portrait.* New York: Abrams, 2005.

Gonzalez, Victoria. *Radical Women in Latin America.* University Park, PA: Pennsylvania State University Press, 2001.

Kirk, Robin. *More Terrible than Death: Drugs, Violence, and America's War in Colombia.* New York: Public Affairs, 2004.

Miller, Francesca. *Latin American Women and the Search for Social Justice.* Lebanon, NH: UPNE, 1991.

Murray, Pam. *Women and Gender in Modern Latin America.* New York and London: Routledge, 2014.

Navarro, Marysa, and Virginia Sanchez Korrol. *Women in Latin America and the Caribbean.* Bloomington, IN: Indiana University Press.

Sloan, Kathryn A. *Women's Roles in Latin America and the Caribbean.* Santa Barbara, CA: Greenwood, 2011.

10

POLITICAL INSTABILITY AND RELATIONS WITH THE UNITED STATES

The North Americans are always among us even when they ignore us or turn their backs on us. Their shadow covers the whole hemisphere. It is the shadow of a giant. And . . . this giant . . . is a great fellow of kind disposition, if a bit simple, who ignores his own strength and who we can fool most of the time, but whose wrath could destroy us.

Octavio Paz

I don't see why we need to stand by and watch a country go communist due to the irresponsibility of its own people.

Henry Kissinger

Political Instability

Latin American politics during the twentieth century were often unstable, violent, and authoritarian. Interestingly, these political tendencies all took place in countries labeled as presidential democracies, most of which shared governmental structures based—loosely or specifically—on the government of the United States. And worst of all, even though presidents and legislatures are normally elected by the populace of the country, Latin American presidential regimes often reverted into dictatorships where leaders set aside the constitutions of their countries and ruled as authoritarian despots.

During the last three decades of the twentieth century, Latin America went through a barrage of political instability that resulted in the collapse of nearly 15 different governments. Interestingly, only two of these disruptions were the result of coups, and both of these coups failed. Instead, presidential incumbents lost their power in more-or-less non-violent ways. Furthermore, the close proximity of the United States to Latin America has meant that regime change in Latin America has been closely monitored, supervised, and in some cases instigated by the US to ensure stable transfers of power. As a result of US policy in the Western Hemisphere, most of the regime collapses and transfers of power in Latin America have come about through actions that only appear democratic.

Political instability resulted not only from corrupt leaders, but also from inflation, economic stagnation, debt (both foreign and domestic), unemployment, and occasional financial crises. Furthermore, Latin American countries, accustomed to strong presidents who ruled through autocratic means and accomplished many things, often saw presidents who ruled through more "democratic" means as weak and in need of replacement (Llanos and Marsteintredet 2010: 6). Street protests, legislative rebellion, and political scandal all played a role in causing political instability in Latin American nations.

During the last decades of the twentieth century, these crises were temporarily solved by the occasional resignation of presidents under severe pressure from their congressional leaders and their public's sentiment. Interestingly, these resignations did not overtly imply the use of military force as in previous decades in Latin America. And although the military did get involved in the removal of some presidents, its support did not take the form of an outright coup, but rather support for the opposition party in congress and as a validation of the protests of the civilian population. It is increasingly clear that Latin American legislatures are becoming more powerful. Presidents are progressively seen as lightning rods for negative political sentiments, and the ousting of an influential leader is only a temporary solution to keep the peace.

US–Latin American Relations

One of the bitter realities for most Latin American nations has been the fact that they share the Western Hemisphere with the most powerful nation on earth, the United States. And even though this situation has certain advantages for Latin America, there are also significant disadvantages as well. Some of the benefits of the relationship between the United States and Latin America include: increased access to trade on more favorable terms; military protection from hostile forces inside and outside a country; grant money and loans for development; and military and political training for the military and leadership. But the disadvantages outweigh the positives in many ways including: frequent US military interventions; mediated or pressured political interventions and coups; economic hegemony; and, at lease from some perspectives, social and cultural domination.

US–Latin American relations politically began in 1823 with the issuing of the Monroe Doctrine in the US. Relations between the two regions did take place prior to 1823, but these instances of interaction were half-hearted, unofficial, or even surreptitious. The Monroe Doctrine, as it has come to be known, was actually part of the State of the Union Address delivered by President James

Monroe in 1823. In his speech he argued that as far as European nations were concerned, the Western Hemisphere was off limits for further intervention or colonization. Those nations such as England and Spain that still had territories in the hemisphere could keep them, but no new acquisitions could be made. Most European nations laughed at the notion of a US president telling them what they could and could not do, and France in particular balked at the conditions of the Monroe Doctrine on a couple of memorable occasions, such as its conquest of Mexico in the middle of the nineteenth century.

By the turn of the twentieth century, the United States involved itself more and more in the affairs of the Latin American nations. In 1904, President Theodore Roosevelt delivered his own address, which is today referred to as the Roosevelt Corollary to the Monroe Doctrine. Roosevelt argued that not only did the Monroe Doctrine designate the Western Hemisphere as free from European control of manipulation, but that the Doctrine also gave the United States the right to a "hands-on" policy in the hemisphere. The consequences of this hands-on policy were staggering. Between 1901 and 1933, the United States used its military to invade Latin American nations nearly the same number of times that it had sent troops into Latin America during the entire nineteenth century. Theodore Roosevelt alone was responsible for more than 20 different military interventions in countries such as Panama, Colombia, Cuba, Nicaragua, Honduras, and the Dominican Republic, to name a few.

The United States earned such a negative reputation for meddling in the affairs of Latin American states that in 1933 President Franklin D. Roosevelt issued a reversal of US procedure in the region that earned the moniker "The Good Neighbor Policy." Under this new strategy, the United States pledged that it would not use its military for overt intervention in Latin American countries. However, if Latin American politicians believed the US was simply going to walk away from all influence in their affairs, they were sorely mistaken. Where the US had used its military in the past, it now tried to influence governments in more subtle ways such as through electoral oversight, investments of capital, international corporations, and the overt actions of the CIA. Following World War II, the Western Hemisphere was plunged into a sense of apprehension over what was perceived as the increasing proliferation of communism.

Sometimes this period in the history of the hemisphere (1950s through 1970s) is called the Era of the National Security States. Over these decades, left-wing insurgencies increased dramatically throughout Latin America, and the US sent military advisors to train Latin American military leaders in guerrilla warfare tactics and counterinsurgency. In many cases, the militaries of these Latin American countries defeated left-leaning guerrilla fighters after long periods of fighting, and then established powerful right-wing military-supported dictatorial governments that enjoyed the support of the US. The United States believed that if conservative regimes were in power in Latin American countries, these countries would be less likely to turn to communism.

The policies of the national security states in Latin America showed a remarkable lack of concern for human rights violations. One analogy that fits this time period is that of a scale. If the scale is tipped too far in one direction by the political establishment—in this case to the right—the obvious reaction for the populace is to pull the scale in the other direction—the left. Many historians have contemplated the rise of communist guerrilla movements in Central and South America throughout the years of the Cold War. It is likely that countries and insurgency movements that appeared left-leaning were just reacting to heavy-handed right-wing governments, and were therefore less ideologically interested in the underpinnings of Marxist-communist theoretical dialectics. Left-wing revolutions occurred throughout the hemisphere in many countries including Brazil, Argentina, Chile, Bolivia, Peru, Guatemala, Mexico, Nicaragua, the Dominican Republic, and El Salvador. But since the US was trying not to use its military in an overt display of force in the hemisphere, the US government resorted to undercover operations by the CIA in Chile, Guatemala, and other locations.

Chile

In 1958, a left-wing socialist named Salvador Allende began to build his political reputation and attract supporters in Chile. He wanted to run for president but was actively barred from becoming a candidate by the military establishment. In 1964 he did run for president of Chile and lost. The United States watched the situation closely and even contributed funds to the campaigns of the right-wing candidates running against him. Allende ran again in 1970 and won the presidency by a very slim margin. After the election, Allende began to implement changes that were positive for the poor and working classes in Chile. However, the US became more and more certain that he was a communist and therefore had to be removed from power.

The Nixon government cut off economic aid to Chile, which quickly led to economic stagnation in the country. This affected people in businesses, education, and the military, all of whom voiced their frustrations to Allende. He also began to lose support from the populace, who knew nothing about the role of the US in Chile's financial struggles. On September 11, 1973, Allende's chief of staff, General Augusto Pinochet, organized and carried out a military coup that removed Allende from power.

During the coup, Allende locked himself in the presidential palace and Pinochet's forces eventually stormed the building. Allende died during the fighting, and Pinochet later claimed that Allende had committed suicide.

By June 1974, Pinochet had named himself dictator of the nation. He implemented a severe eradication campaign to get rid of all left-wing activity in Chile. Thousands of people disappeared or were killed and tortured. Civil rights were revoked; censorship, surveillance, and martial law were now the status quo. For the rest of Pinochet's time in power, Chile stagnated economically even though it relied heavily upon US financial support. Eventually the conditions in Chile came to light, but not until after years of secrecy and governmental cover-ups that came from the highest levels of the US State Department. In the 1970s, an American reported named Charles Horman, who was living in Chile, wrote for a left-wing Chilean newspaper named *FIN* (*Fuente de Información Norteamericano, North American Information Source*). In September 1973, Horman disappeared, and his wife, father, and others spent much time in Chile and the United States trying to locate him, or his body, by going through tremendous amounts of governmental red tape and obfuscation by the Chilean regime. Today, declassified CIA documents make it clearer what happened to Horman during the Pinochet coup. Horman was visiting the city of Viña del Mar, which was, unbeknown to him, a central location for US troops during the coup. Horman was detained by the Chilean military for digging too deep into the coup, and finding information that apparently linked the US government to events in Chile. Horman was eventually killed in a football stadium with thousands of other political and social undesirables and activists. Horman's body was eventually shipped back to his family in the United States, nearly a year after his death, and his family was charged $900 for the cost of transporting his body to the US from Chile.

Guatemala

Like Chile, Guatemala experienced a left-wing revolution associated with a political leader—in this case, Colonel Jacobo Árbenz—and a subsequent US orchestrated military coup. Árbenz became the president of Guatemala in 1951. He was a military officer and the US believed he was their man in the Guatemalan government. Árbenz had previously served as the minister of defense under the previous president. But after his election, he surprised Guatemalans and US politicians alike when he appointed several prominent communists from the Guatemalan Communist Party to fill cabinet-level positions. Then, he surprised even more people when he issued Decree 900, which implemented one of the largest agrarian reforms in Central American history. In 1952, Árbenz nationalized more than 200000 acres of fallow land that belonged to the United Fruit Company (UFCO). UFCO was a Boston-based fruit company that specialized in the growth and transportation of bananas from Central America to the United States. UFCO used a policy of land grabbing whereby the company would purchase more land than it could cultivate. This accomplished two purposes: first, it meant that the land for future UFCO cultivation did not need to be acquired later when prices might be higher; second, if UFCO owned the land, even if it was not being used, it meant that the competing fruit companies could not acquire or use the land for their own banana operations.

When Árbenz expropriated the UFCO acres of land, he then distributed the land to Guatemalan farmers and agriculturalists for the production of corn, beans, and other agrarian products. UFCO was furious and appealed to the US State Department to help them regain their lands. Árbenz took as his example the earlier expropriation of US oilfields in Mexico. In the 1930s, Mexican president Lázaro Cárdenas had nationalized oil production in Mexico, much of which was owned and operated by the US. In the end, Mexico had paid the US the worth of the lands and equipment and the US effectively walked away. Árbenz believed that a similar solution could be reached in his country of Guatemala, and he even offered to pay UFCO for the lands he had taken.

But this time the US was not interested in simply walking away. Two individuals especially influenced policy on handling the UFCO situation in Guatemala: John Foster Dulles and his brother Allan Dulles. Allan Dulles had been an UFCO attorney and member of the UFCO board of directors, and was now the director of the CIA. His brother John Foster Dulles was the Secretary of State. Soon, a coup was launched that was aimed at the regime of President Árbenz. An invasion of Guatemala from Honduras, made up of Guatemalan and Honduran rebels, backed by CIA support, was staged. Planes flew over Guatemala City dropping propaganda leaflets in support of the invasion. Árbenz grounded his air force after false allegations that his pilots were defecting to Mexico. The Guatemalan legislature and presidential cabinet panicked and forced Árbenz to resign the presidency. Árbenz went into exile in Cuba, and the new president of Guatemala, Carlos Castillo Armas, negotiated a return of all UFCO lands and equipment back to the banana company.

The results of the coup were dramatic. Guatemala reverted to full dictatorial control, complete with repression of Native American Guatemalans, censorship, assassinations, disappearances, ethnic cleansing, and other atrocities. As many as one million Maya Indians fled into Mexico and Central American nations attempting to get away from the brutality. This 40-year-long civil war is referred to as *Las Ruinas* (The Ruins). And, as in El Salvador later in the late 1970s, it led to the politicizing of the Catholic Church as priests and bishops spoke out against the violence. In 1992, a 33-year-old Maya woman named Rigoberta Menchu won the Nobel Peace Prize for bringing to light on a world stage the events of this tragedy, and in 1998, Bishop Juan Gerardi was murdered for speaking out against the Guatemalan army. He was bludgeoned to death with a piece of cement resembling a cinder block.

Conclusions

US–Latin American relations is a vibrant area of study for American and Latin American historians alike. The relationship between these areas of the hemisphere has shaped much of the hemispheric policy over the past 200 years. Sometimes this relationship has been positive and mutually beneficial to both areas. Sometimes, however, one side or the other has gained while the other has lost resources, lost face, or lost control over its own destiny. The political instability that at times has afflicted many Latin American countries seems to have been an impetus for US intervention in these countries, and from the perspective of the United States, these interventions have been calculated to preserve peace, prosperity, and accord in the hemisphere. But from Latin America's viewpoint, US intervention has been a one-way street that benefited the US while leaving Latin American nations financially, politically, and militarily weak and vulnerable. In either case, Latin America made significant progress over the course of the twentieth century in terms of self-sufficiency in terms of economic and political self-determinism. It can be hoped that the positive trends that were in place at the end of the twentieth century will continue to mature in the region, while the negative aspects that have led to political instability will decline.

Filmography

Political instability in modern Latin American countries was endemic during the last half of the twentieth century. Governmental regimes adopted courses of violence and human rights violations, while the US supported right-wing dictatorships in the name of preventing the proliferation of communism in the Western Hemisphere. Three films are presented here that deal with issues related to these events. *Missing* (1982), directed by Constantine Costa-Gavras, *Salvador* (1986), directed by Oliver Stone, and *The Official Story* (*La Historia Oficial*, 1985), from director Luis Puenzo, all outline different elements of this tumultuous time. *Missing* presents Chile during the early 1970s in the wake of the rise to power of General Augusto Pinochet and his military junta. *Salvador* looks at the relationship between the US and El Salvador during the 1980s civil war in that country during the presidency of Ronald Reagan in the US. *The Official Story* takes place in Argentina following the Dirty War of the 1970s and 1980s when the military government was toppled and political prisoners were released. All three films deal with politically sensitive topics and all are depressing in their way. But these stories are essential to understanding the political and military elements in many Latin American countries in the latter half of the twentieth century.

Missing *(1982)*

Constantine Costa-Gavras' film *Missing* (1992) takes place in Chile in September 1973. The film chronicles the final days of American reporter Charles Horman who lived in Chile with his wife at that time. He worked as a writer for a left-wing newspaper named *FIN*. The film shows many signs of the new military government's occupation of the cities of Chile. For example, military soldiers carry books to bonfires and burn them. There is an imposed curfew, and people are not permitted to be on the streets after dark under penalty of death. Women are not permitted to wear pants in public. Dead bodies are occasionally found lying in the streets where they have fallen. The casualness of the violence in the film is chilling. Gunfire erupts throughout the film in daylight and at night. At the beginning of the film, the characters jump whenever they hear gunfire. By the end of the film they do not jump any longer.

Prior to the military coup that took place in Chile in September 1973, Charles Horman had been visiting the coastal city of Viña del Mar. The hotel where he was staying was full of US military personnel. When he finally gets back to the capital, he knows a lot more about the involvement of the US in the coup than he did before his trip. Horman returns to the capital and is reunited with his wife. But a couple of days later, she returns home to find that he has been taken by the military and their house has been roughly searched.

When Horman is reported missing, his father, Ed (Jack Lemmon) in New York, tries to find out what happened, and to recover his son. He visits with senators, representatives, an ambassador, and individuals in the State Department. They all tell him more or less the same thing, that they cannot help him. After several frustrating meetings Ed decides to go to Chile to find his son himself. He meets Beth (Sissy Spacek), Horman's wife, at a hotel, and they both begin to search for Horman together. They are soon informed that Horman must be hiding because his body has not turned up anywhere.

They attempt to talk to the neighbors and ask them what they saw on the day that Horman disappeared. One of the neighbors says that she saw Horman taken out of the house by military men and driven away in a truck. Others tell them that Horman was driven to the national stadium. As Ed and Beth tighten their search, they visit a hospital in an attempt to find Horman among the unidentified patients. Ed asks what Horman might have done in order to get

FIGURE 10.1 Sissy Spacek and Jack Lemmon in *Missing* (1982, Universal Pictures).

arrested. He is told quite frankly, "You Americans. You always assume you must do something before you can be arrested."

Eventually Beth and Ed enter the national stadium where individuals have gathered to look for relatives or wait for loved ones to come and retrieve them. After making an impassioned plea to the crowd of people, they go into the basements to look for Horman among the dead bodies. While they do not find Horman, they do discover the previously unidentified body of Frank Teruggi, one of the other American journalists who worked with Horman on *FIN*, and they realize that Horman is most likely dead too. Ultimately, Ed meets a man who golfs with a member of the ambassador's team. That man says that the ambassador believes Horman was killed in the stadium in mid-September. Ed speculates that it wouldn't have been possible to kill an American unless the US was in some way complicit. He is told that the US presence in Chile is to protect the 3000 American businesses that make money in Chile. Ultimately, individuals who work at the American Embassy in Santiago confirm that Horman is indeed dead.

Ed and Beth prepare to leave the country. They are informed by these same embassy employees that Horman's body will be shipped home in a few days. They are also told that they will have to pay for the shipping fees themselves. When they return to the States, Ed files suits against 11 different US government officials including secretary of state Henry Kissinger. The body of Charles Horman finally arrives in the United States nearly a year later, making an autopsy impossible. Finally, all the suits that Ed Horman brought against government officials were ultimately dismissed.

The film *Missing* does a very good job of accurately portraying the tense situation in Chile during the 1973 coup. The film is very violent, but Costa-Gavras made the decision to "portray" the violence offscreen, implying that it was there, but not presenting it to the viewer. This lends a sense of tension and horror in the viewer who does not know what is going to happen next. In 1982, *New York Times* film critic Vincent Canby observed this when he wrote, "*Missing* . . . contains several harrowing scenes of violence, as well as a sequence in a Santiago morgue that could inspire nightmares." Because the film is strongly based on actual events, it drew intense criticism from the US and Chilean governments. At the beginning of the film, the following statement is read by Jack Lemmon: "This film is based on a true story. The incidents and facts are documented. Some of the names have been changed to protect the innocent and also to protect the film." Finally, Costa-Gavras achieved the sense that the coup in Chile brought the lives of ordinary Chileans to a halt. He accomplishes this through deft work with the camera, the commanding performances by Lemmon and Spacek, and the haunting atmosphere that pervades the film. In a way, Missing captures the sentiment so aptly described by Lars Schoultz when he wrote that the Chilean coup was "a slow-motion mortification without end" (Schoultz 1998: 361).

Salvador *(1986)*

Oliver Stone's film *Salvador* (1986) takes place in the Central American country of El Salvador in 1980. The film focuses on the historical journalist Richard Boyle (James Woods), a writer who can't find a job because he is something of a screw-up. In order to get some work, he and a friend (James Belushi) drive all the way from the US to El Salvador. He hopes to get some photographs of the Salvadoran guerrillas that he can sell to a news magazine. He and his friend eventually meet another reporter named John Cassady who tells Boyle that El Salvador is too dangerous for reporters.

Boyle eventually finds and photographs a dump of dead bodies. He then travels to the capitol, San Salvador where he hopes to help people who are searching for their dead relatives. US President Ronald Reagan is shown on television giving a speech on the proliferation of communism in Central America. The film develops the fact that the military government of El Salvador is pleased with the White House and its support of the efforts to eradicate communism in the country.

Boyle continued to attempt to make contacts that can help him get a job, and to beg for money from people he knows. He eventually gets a contract with a publisher in Atlanta for some photographs. He also tries to get official papers for his Salvadoran girlfriend so that he can take her out of the country to protect her from the violence. In an attempt to get permission to marry her, so that they can get the papers they need, they go to see Archbishop Óscar Romero. Romero is the outspoken leader of the Catholic Church in El Salvador, and he is actively speaking out against the military government and the violence and oppression that they are imposing on the people (Óscar Romero is discussed in greater detail in Chapter 11). When they encounter Romero, he is preaching a sermon about the disappeared and the oppression of the military on the poor who are believed to be communists because of their poverty. The film shows the famous speech that Romero delivers right before he is assassinated. Romero asks the military to stop the repression. After his murder, the army attempts to prevent people from leaving and in the ensuing confusion, Boyle has his camera confiscated.

The film continues portraying scenes of violence and subjugation of the poor by the military. A van full of Red Cross workers and nuns is stopped, whereupon the nuns are raped and then shot. Boyle who is there is beaten and almost killed as well. He attempts to reason with the military men, telling them that there isn't a communist revolution in El Salvador, just a peasant revolution and a civil war. He argues that the war is being perpetuated by the military that won't leave the peasantry alone. He goes on to talk about human rights violations and the open US support of the right-wing military dictatorship. The film then moves to the guerrilla opposition leaders who are raising an FMLN flag. The Farabundo Martí National Liberation Front (FMLN) was an overarching guerrilla movement that organized and coordinated the fighters and peasant revolutionaries in El Salvador. Today, the FMLN has become more of a political party and even holds several seats in the Salvadoran government.

Eventually Boyle is able to get his girlfriend and her two children out of El Salvador. But Boyle remains in El Salvador, where he is again beaten and has his camera film confiscated and ruined once again. On a bus in the US, Boyle's girlfriend and her children are taken off the bus by the border patrol, indicating that their escape to the US has failed. Finally Boyle is arrested and taken to an unknown fate while John Cassady tries to smuggle their photographs out of the country.

The value of *Salvador* is in the depictions of the violence that permeated and plagued El Salvador in the early 1980s, the repression of the military government on the poor, and the work of reporters like Boyle who attempt to convey the violence to the world. Unfortunately, *Salvador* is weighed down by director Stone's mixture of the truth with fiction. Many aspects of the film are absolutely true, but other aspects are fictional such as Boyle's attempt to get his girlfriend out of the country, and the character of Cassady who seems to be included in the film to move the plot along, to give Boyle information, and to bring the film to some sort of conclusion.

In 1986, Roger Ebert reviewed *Salvador* and came to the following conclusion, "*Salvador* is long and disjointed and tries to tell too many stories . . . But the heart of the movie is fascinating. And the heart consists of Woods and Belushi, two losers set adrift in a world they never made, trying to play games by everybody else's rules".

The Official Story (1985)

The Official Story (1985; known originally as *La Historia Oficial*), is an Argentine film that depicts one woman's search for the truth about political prisoners and *los desaparecidos* (the disappeared) in Argentina in the early 1980s. The film won an Oscar for Best Foreign Language Film in 1986. It takes place in Argentina in 1983 in the wake of the so-called Dirty War that perpetuated the dictatorship of Reynaldo Bignone. The Dirty War was a period of time in Argentina's history when the military government killed and disappeared communist guerrillas, arrested political prisoners, and any others who were suspected of being communists. Some have speculated that the number of dead and disappeared could reach as high as 30000 people. In the film, Alicia is a high school history teacher. She and her husband have an adopted daughter named Gaby who is five years old.

One of Alicia's friends visits early in the film and talks about being water-boarded and electrocuted several years earlier. She informs Alicia that some of the women in the detention center were pregnant and their children were taken and sold to others who didn't ask too many questions. Alicia begins to wonder if her daughter Gaby might have been one of these babies.

Alicia starts to question her husband about Gaby's past. He is reticent to speak about it and attempts to get her to change the subject on multiple occasions. In her high school class, Alicia teaches about the history of Argentina. This is an interesting juxtaposition because her students are discussing freedom of speech and of the press. They mention the repression of the current government and how it has dominated the lives of the people for years. Alicia treats these topics as nothing but rumors. She seems to be out of touch with the current history of Argentina and her students are much more politically active than she is.

Finally, Alicia begins to ask some questions of her own. Where have the disappeared gone? Are they working in other locations, or have they been detained like her friend who was tortured? When she leaves the city on one occasion, she sees an outdoor rally, where the Grandmothers of the *Plaza de Mayo* are marching in protest over their relatives who have been disappeared. They carry signs and placards that show photos of their lost relatives. Alicia slowly becomes more and more interested in the history of the disappeared people and what happened to them and their families. Increasingly, she is also troubled by the work her husband does. She doesn't really know what he does at work and has been kept in the dark about how he makes his money. Every time she brings up the question of Gaby's past, he gets angry and won't answer her questions.

At one point in the film, her husband has a verbal bout with his father and brother. He tells them that he knows what side to be on during the revolution and that he is not a loser like they are. It appears that he has had something to do with the establishment of the new government of Argentina, or at lease is complicit in some of the work the government is involved in.

Meanwhile Alicia goes looking for the doctor that gave them Gaby. She also talks to the priest who was there the day Gaby was given to them. Neither will give her any answers and she becomes increasingly troubled at the prospect that perhaps Gaby's biological mother might not have given her up voluntarily. As Alicia grows more obsessive about Gaby's past, she pays less and less attention in her high school classroom, and she and her husband drift further apart as she continues to beleaguer him about whether or not Gaby was the child of a disappeared mother.

Eventually she is approached by a woman who is looking for her lost grand-daughter. She believes that Gaby may be the missing girl. She and Alicia compare photographs and information. The woman has dates of a couple's marriage and pregnancy, and then their disappearance. Alicia brings the woman to her home and announces to her husband that she thinks that this woman is Gaby's grandmother. Her husband becomes furious and, after the woman leaves, Alicia confronts her husband again whereupon he all but confesses that Gaby was indeed the child of a disappeared woman. Then in a burst of violence he beats Alicia brutally.

The Official Story is dark and depressing. It describes the feelings that many had in Argentina during this troubling time in its history. The Dirty War in Argentina was a tragic time when the military controlled the country and carried out acts of terror and brutality against its own people. The Grandmothers of the *Plaza de Mayo* still march to this day and ask for answers to the questions of past human rights violations perpetuated by the Argentine government on the people of Argentina.

Further Reading

Arditti, Rita. *Searching for Life: The Grandmothers of the Plaza de Mayo and the Disappeared Children of Argentina.* Berkeley, CA: University of California Press, 1999.

Brewer, Stewart. *Borders and Bridges: A History of US–Latin American Relations.* Santa Barbara, CA: Praeger, 2006.

Gleijeses, Piero. *Shattered Hope: The Guatemalan Revolution and the United States 1944–1954.* Princeton, NJ: Princeton University Press, 1992.

Llanos, Mariana, and Leiv Marsteintredet. *Presidential Breakdowns in Latin America.* London: Palgrave, 2010.

Menchu, Rigoberta. *I, Rigoberta Menchu.* London: Verso, 2010.

Qureshi, Lubna Z. *Nixon, Kissinger, and Allende: US Involvement in the 1973 Coup in Chile.* Lanham, MD: Lexington Books, 2009.

Schlesinger, Stephen. *Bitter Fruit.* Cambridge, MA: David Rockefeller Center for Latin American Studies, 2005.

Schoultz, Lars. *Beneath the United States: A History of US Policy toward Latin America.* Cambridge, MA: Harvard University Press, 1998.

Stoll, David. *Rogoberta Menchu and the Story of All Poor Guatemalans.* Boulder, CO: Westview Press, 2007.

11
POVERTY, TERRORISM, AND VIOLENCE IN LATIN AMERICA

Brothers, you came from our own people. You are killing your own brothers. Any human order to kill must be subordinate to the law of God, which says, "Thou shalt not kill." No soldier is obliged to obey an order contrary to the law of God. No one has to obey an immoral law. It is time you obeyed your consciences rather than sinful orders. The Church cannot remain silent before such an abomination. In the name of God, in the name of this suffering people whose cry rises to heaven more loudly each day, I implore you, I beg you, I order you: stop the repression!

Archbishop Óscar Romero

Introduction

Throughout the twentieth century, Latin America saw an increase in terrorism, violence, and poverty. In and of themselves, these phenomena have had drastic effects on Latin American communities. Combined, they have wrought havoc and suffering on a large scale in some of Latin America's most needy neighborhoods, cities, and nations. Recent efforts to combat these occurrences have grown out of movements within Latin American nations, and also through aid and support from the governments of the United States and other nations. Currently, the US State Department lists four Latin American organizations as active terrorist movements: the Revolutionary Armed Forces of Colombia (FARC), the United Self-Defense Forces of Colombia (AUC), the National Liberation Army of Colombia (ELN), and the Shining Path of Peru. Other groups have been listed in the past, only to eventually be removed from the list of Latin American terrorist organizations, such as the Manuel Rodríguez Patriotic Front of Chile.

Terrorism and Violence

Terrorism is not a new phenomenon in modern Latin America. In the 1960s in Nicaragua, a left-wing revolutionary organization called the Sandinista National Liberation Front (FSLN), or just Sandinistas for short, began to emerge. By the early 1970s, the Sandinistas began to fight for the rights of the poor people of Nicaragua by kidnapping government officials and presenting demands for change. By 1979, the Sandinistas rose to power in a popular uprising that ousted the sitting government. When the dictator of Nicaragua fled to Miami that year, the Sandinistas took control of Nicaragua and ruled until 1990. The fighting and violence of the revolution left around 50000 Nicaraguans dead. During the 1980s, the Sandinista government fought against a US-funded counterrevolutionary force called the Contras. In 1990, the Sandinistas were toppled from power in a popular election. Since the turn of the twenty-first century, the Sandinistas have returned to power in Nicaragua as a left-wing political party, but many remember the violence and bloodshed of the revolutionary years.

Another powerful terrorist organization in Latin America is called Sendero Luminoso (Shining Path) in Peru. Shining Path also emerged in the 1960s as a product of the Peruvian Communist Party. Largely a student organization at first, Shining Path became popular on college and university campuses in the early 1970s, but by 1980 the movement's leaders ordered the beginning of a militant revolution in Peru. Peasant communities in Peru supported the movement because of its promises of justice against the oppression of the government. Shining Path guerrillas killed government supporters and assassinated political leaders. Throughout the rest of the twentieth century, Shining Path continued to carry out terrorist attacks, bombings, kidnappings, and assassinations. But while these activities have in some instances continued into the twenty-first century, Shining Path's leadership has struggled to maintain power and the number of violent clashes has decreased.

Finally, in Colombia, the Revolutionary Armed Forces of Colombia (FARC) is perhaps the most dangerous terrorist organization in Latin America today. It is estimated that FARC is responsible for nearly 80 percent of all terrorist attacks in the Western Hemisphere.[1] Following the decade-long civil war in Colombia in the 1950s that left more than 300000 people dead, Colombia was in political turmoil. In the chaos and confusion that ensued, FARC was organized in the early 1960s as a guerrilla movement that fought against the weak government. In the 1980s, FARC continued to grow and funded many of its activities through production and sale of coca leaves to bordering nations and foreign countries. During the remaining years of the twentieth century, FARC and the Columbian government attempted to reconcile, all while the acts of terrorism continued. In the years since the turn of the twenty-first century, FARC has remained active in kidnappings, assassinations, and drug smuggling. Recently, however, FARC agreed to surrender many of its hostages, and its numbers have dwindled from more than 10000 active participants to around 8000, but the conflict continues.

Of course there have been other, smaller terrorist organizations and groups in Latin American history from time to time that have enacted extreme violence and caused untold pain and suffering. The United States has involved itself repeatedly in efforts to aid Latin American nations in combatting terrorism within the borders of Latin American countries. Economic sanctions, anti-terrorism and law enforcement training, and combatting the production and distribution of illegal drugs are all strategies that have been utilized by the US to aid Latin American countries in eradicating these terrorist elements from within their borders. And, since 9/11, the US and Latin American countries have maintained increasing levels of hemispheric cooperation in combatting terrorist movements.[2]

Poverty

During the twenty-first century, poverty will continue to be one of the most critical challenges faced in Latin America. The chasm between the wealthy and the poor in Latin America continues to widen, and access to resources to sustain life for the very poor is becoming more and more tenuous. Undernourishment and limited access to clean water and sufficient food increases the prevalence of malnutrition and disease among poor communities in Latin American nations. And, despite the huge gap in income between the wealthy and the poor, it is estimated that while the poor spend most of their meager income on food and shelter, the wealthy spend most of their money on conspicuous consumption; the purchase of unneeded luxury items. Other factors that perpetuate poverty in Latin America include illegal drug-related production and consumption, internal and regional hostilities, migration between countries and communities, population growth, corrupt political systems, and insufficient development and distribution of food, clothing, shelter, and medicine.

The effect of poverty in Latin America is substantial. Poverty is one of the leading factors in perpetuating unhealthy populations. Poor communities are more likely to suffer from malnutrition, dehydration, starvation, and disease than wealthier populations. Infant mortality increases and life expectancy decreases as a result of lack of sufficient medical procedures and supplies. And finally, crime rates increase dramatically in poor communities as people struggle to find the resources that they need, and resort to violence and crime to secure the things needed to sustain life.

Clean, sufficient housing is another missing aspect of life for the poor in Latin America. Slums in Latin American countries go by many names: *villas*, *favelas*, *barrios*, *pueblos*, and *colonies* are all types of poverty-stricken slums in Latin America. But they are all breeding grounds for disease, malnutrition, health problems, crime, violence, and corruption. Drug abuse, prostitution, human trafficking, and murder are but a few of the daily realities the poor face in their communities.

Perhaps unsurprisingly, alcohol and illegal drugs are more easily obtained in slums than one might expect. Residents may see these substances as escape mechanisms, but the results are even more tragic. Physical and psychological addiction only exacerbates the problems of poverty in the slums as incomes are lost and squandered, lives are lost and disrupted through, death, suicide, and violence, and families are broken up and children are left to fend for themselves when their parents die. Additionally, the quality of the illegal drugs that people are purchasing in these conditions is very poor as dealers try to stretch their supplies in order to generate more revenue.

Finally, education opportunities dwindle in cases of extreme poverty. And, while education has the ability to elevate individuals from the crippling effects of poverty, the very poor are the least likely to obtain sufficient levels of education to do them much good. Even in locations where educational opportunities exist, families and individuals who live in extreme poverty cannot afford to pay for schooling because of lack of funds, and also because they must spend their time finding ways to survive instead of getting a rudimentary education. The long-term results are violence, crime, pregnancy, and negligence to name only a few.

Combating poverty in Latin America has been attempted in various ways over the decades. The several factors that result in poverty are not easy to correct individually, let alone in concert. And even in countries with relatively high levels of economic stability, poverty remains a problem that must be dealt with. Combinations of external (foreign-funded industrialization and improved infrastructure, and foreign-trained professionals) and internal (waste removal, mobile food and water programs, social welfare programs, and mobile health services) measures can and do provide some relief, but corruption in the government frequently prevents relief and aid monies from getting where they should go.

In Central America, conditions are particularly bad. When compared to the other nations of Latin America, Central American countries are extremely poor, small, and have been the centers of life-threatening violence. The way Central America developed after independence from Spain had a profound effect on its growth and progress. In order to survive, Central American nations relied on exporting cash crops to wealthy nations such as the United States and the United Kingdom. Some of the commodities that have been exported from Central America over the years include coffee, sugar, chocolate, and bananas. In fact, bananas played such an important role in the economies of some Central American countries that they earned the moniker "banana republics." Because of this cash crop mentality, during the nineteenth century, Central America developed a plantation-style mindset with a very class-conscious division between the elite, the poverty-stricken, and the ethnic and racial minorities. During the twentieth century, Central America did not overcome the division and today the very wealthy rule the nations of the region while the poor continue to suffer some of the worst conditions in the hemisphere.

Central America has the distinction of being the region in the Western Hemisphere with the most intense US intervention and military presence in history. During the Cold War, the US feared the proliferation of communism in the Western Hemisphere, and following the Cuban Revolution and Fidel Castro's rise to power, policymakers in the US began to use the military and the CIA to quash the spread of communism in Central America.

El Salvador

El Salvador, the smallest of the Central American countries, went through a variety of problems during the twentieth century including overpopulation and violence, economic immaturity, and racial intolerance. The economy of El Salvador rested on the production and sale of a monocrop of coffee. In the 1930s, the government seized indigenous lands in order to increase coffee production. When the Indians protested, the military slaughtered thousands of them in 1932 in the massacre that came to be called *La Matanza* (The Killing). More than 30000 indigenous people from poor communities were killed and the violence led unavoidably to more instability in El Salvador through the mid twentieth century. The results of *La Matanza* were astonishing but not unexpected: indigenous dress was wiped out; indigenous languages were abandoned; indigenous cultural traditions became extinct; and Indian society all but disappeared as Indians struggled to vanish into the Mestizo population of El Salvador.

In 1980, El Salvador plunged into the massive 12-year civil war that devastated the country and resulted in the deaths of more than 70000 people. The predominant guerrilla force in El Salvador during the war was the Farabundo Martí National Liberation Front (FMLN). In the early 1980s, the Salvadoran military murdered 18 Catholic priests who had voiced their support of the insurgency against the government, and spoken out against the intense violence that pervaded the country. One of these priests was the archbishop of El Salvador, Óscar Romero who was gunned down as he said Mass, as described in Chapter 10.

Father Romero had used his pulpit to support the poor, indigenous, Mestizos, students, and other downtrodden populations who were being abused by the state. Bible study was combined with social activism and poor Salvadorans came away with the message that God was a god of justice who loved the poor and abhorred violence. Because of their activism, priests became targets of government retribution, and the government distributed flyers that said, "Be a patriot, kill a priest!" Romero had used his weekly radio addresses to condemn the government for their abuses of power. He also organized strikes, sit-ins, and public demonstrations.

Archbishop Romero's death had vast repercussions in El Salvador. In the early 1980s, five major guerrilla groups united under a single banner called the FMLN and in January 1981, they launched one of the worst civil wars in Central American history. As mentioned above, the fighting lasted on and off until 1992 when a ceasefire was negotiated and the FMLN became an official political party in El Salvador.

Brazil

In most regards, Brazil is as different as can be from Central America. But many of the problems that Central American countries and communities have faced have also been problematic in areas of Brazil. Some of the worse conditions in South America are found in the *favela* communities of Rio de Janeiro and other Brazilian cities. *Favelas* are unofficial communities that are erected outside cities without the support or even consent of city officials. They have existed as parasites on the outskirts of Brazilian cities since the end of the 1800s, and some of them have become incredibly large. Janice Perlman, in her book *Favela*, describes them as squatter settlements, shantytowns, and irregular settlements on the peripheries of (an in some cases actually inside) the city limits. By the 1960s they were detested, but were also more-or-less accepted as part of the landscape.[3] At first the *favelas* developed along foothills and near the coasts on territory that cities had not yet encompassed. Then as time went on, the *favelas* grew up the sides of the hills in a vertical form of growth. As they continued to grow, city governments became more and more inept at stopping their progress.

Poverty in Brazil's slums is among the worst in the world. The absence of running water, electricity, transportation, legal commerce, and government regulation make living in the *favelas* dangerous on many levels. The lack of oversight in *favela* life and development has led to the growth of small-scale functioning "governments" and "police" forces inside the *favelas*. These institutions are usually provided by those who have the means in the slums, namely the drug dealers and crime bosses. Finally, the population density in Brazil's favelas is astonishing. In Rio's famous *favela*, Cidade de Deus (City of God), the population density is around 38000 people per square mile. Other slums such as Alemão (Germany) and Jacarezinho (Little Jacaré, named after the Jacaré river), both have levels of near 60000 inhabitants per 1.5 square miles.

Conclusions

Crime, poverty, violence, and terrorism are daily problems in many locations of Latin America today. Efforts to combat the effects of these issues are ongoing and international aid is also expended in these areas to help them eradicate or at least contain these evils. But the reality is that the very poor in Latin America continue to suffer, and terrorist organizations continue to pursue their agendas. Funding, education, and real policing of communities are all effective methods for combatting these issues. But as long as corruption at the city and state level continues, the means to fully exterminate these problems will continue to be an elusive solution to a terrible reality.

Filmography

Many different films could be showcased in this chapter on terrorism, violence, and poverty in Latin America. The three presented here represent not only the wide geography of these conditions in Latin America—from Mexico, through Central America, and to Brazil—but also the uniform struggle of the poor in countries where violence and corruption disrupt their lives. *Romero* portrays the violence in El Salvador in the 1970s and 1980s, highlighting the role the Catholic Church played in fighting for the rights of the peasants who were targeted by the government as communist sympathizers and subversives. *City of God* illustrates the rampant violence and poverty in the slums of Brazil by focusing on the *favela* named Cidade de Deus near Rio de Janeiro. The drugs, poverty, and violence there threaten the lives of the inhabitants daily. Finally, *Men With Guns* examines the gulf between the wealthy and the poor in countries where violence and terrorism are rampant. Often, the affluent in these countries know little or nothing about the atrocities committed within the borders of their own nations in the name of national security. Each of these films contributes to the modern history of brutality in Latin America, and the desire for an end to the suffering and exploitation of the innocent.

Romero *(1989)*

The film *Romero* was released in 1989. Director John Duigan's film portrays the violence and corruption that filled the government of El Salvador in the late 1970s and early 1980s. At the end of the 1970s, the people of El Salvador were still locked in a class struggle; wealthy against poor, and white against indigenous.

As the film opens, Fathers Óscar Romero (Raúl Juliá) and Rutilio Grande (Richard Jordan) view voters protesting the military government and the apparent corruption in fixing elections in the country. As Father Grande becomes more agitated about the situation, Father Romero tells him to calm down and not act like a subversive. The film does a very good job portraying Romero in the late 1970s as a priest who is not very connected to the acts of injustice taking place in El Salvador. Instead, he spends his time and energies with books and scholarly activities, oblivious to the political and military corruption and violence in his country. As the film progresses, Duigan portrays Father Romero's transformation into a priest who not only begins to champion the rights of the poor and indigenous of El Salvador, but also one who collides head-on with the military government over its corruption and abuse of basic human rights.

As the election in El Salvador takes place, many poor farmers travel to polling places to cast their votes. But the military blockades the roads, preventing the people from arriving in time to cast their ballots. The pretext that the military gives is that the countryside is full of guerrilla fighters who are trying to sabotage the election, and they cannot let the people proceed for their own safety. When Father Romero and Father Grande arrive on the scene to protest the people's detainment, the soldiers riddle the bus that carried the peasants with bullets. The priests then decide to walk with the farmers to the polling place instead so they can cast their votes. This is the beginning of Romero's transformation into an advocate for the people.

Eventually, Óscar Romero is selected to be the archbishop of El Salvador for the Catholic Church. In the film, Romero has been selected because he is seen as weak; a person who can be easily manipulated and who will not make problems in the Church or for the government. Soon after his selection, a group of people protest the actions of the government, and the military fires on them, killing several. When archbishop Romero finds out, he is troubled, but does nothing. The tipping point for Romero comes when Father Grande and some individuals in his car are gunned down by soldiers dressed as guerrillas. Romero holds a funeral for the slain individuals, including Father Grande, a peasant farmer, and a young boy. Romero is concerned that Grande was too politically active for a priest, but he understands that the responsibility of priests is to protect and minister to the poor.

The film shows the violence that was perpetrated by the military government on the poor and indigenous, including kidnappings, ransoms, and dead bodies dumped in city landfills. Archbishop Romero realizes that he cannot remain oblivious any longer; he must take a stand and choose a side. One of the final acts that solidifies Romero's position on government violence is the capture and torture of another priest who the military accuse of being a subversive. Romero decides to visit the president-elect of El Salvador, who is also a general in the military. When he is denied an interview, he simply walks into a private meeting and begins to speak out against the violence. He is told in no uncertain terms that priests must stay out of politics.

Soon, troops begin occupying and closing churches in retaliation for the priests getting involved with the people. As Romero enters a church to retrieve the Eucharist, he is taunted and driven away. The soldiers mock him and desecrate the church with gunfire. Later, Romero is detained on the street by another group of soldiers. They "search" him for weapons by stripping his robes from him. Romero takes all these indignities in stride and continues his crusade for the poor of El Salvador.

Archbishop Romero eventually begins using the radio to broadcast his message throughout the country. He calls upon the military and the government to end the violence and stop the killing. In his dialog he condemns the violence and the individuals who carry out the aggressive acts. His famous quote on this occasion is presented at the beginning of this chapter. The film concludes with Romero's assassination in 1980. He was shot during a Mass and the assassins have never been brought to justice.

Romero as a film succeeds in portraying the violence and indignity that was suffered in El Salvador in the 1970s and 1980s, and the role that the Church played in defending the rights of the poor and indigenous populations. Although Romero's assassination was inflammatory and provocative, he was not the only priest killed by the establishment for opposing the rule of the current regime. The film portrays the persecution and abuse of other priests who are associates of Romero, and their eventual radicalization against the government as they are persuaded to take up arms to defend the people. However, Romero's death came to symbolize the fight for justice against violence and oppression in Central America, and the struggle against corrupt governments and military dictators.

Romero is a very poignant piece of film that portrays the transformation of Archbishop Romero from an introverted, oblivious priest, to a political activist who championed the cause of the poor against the might of the military regime. Nevertheless, the *New York Times* review of the film states that "Raul Julia is persuasive without being very moving," and "*Romero* is more important as the brief, considerably simplified biography of a heroic man than as cinema." And in a similar light, Roger Ebert noted that "The film has a good heart . . . [but] doesn't stir many passions, and it seems more sorrowing than angry. Romero was a good man, he did what his heart told him to do and he died for his virtues. It is a story told every day in Latin America" (http://rogerebert.com).

Cidade de Deus *(2002)*

In 2002, *Cidade de Deus* (*City of God*) was released. Directed by Fernando Meirelles and Kátia Lund, it chronicles life in the *favelas* of Brazil. The film was based on a previously published book of the same name written by Paulo Lins, which portrayed historical events in the favela Cidade de Deus on the outskirts of Rio de Janeiro. *Cidade de Deus* is a very violent film that does not shy away from portraying the ugly side of living in a *favela*. Unfortunately, by the end of the film, the viewer is less and less shocked, and more complacent about the violence and even comes to accept it as part of everyday life in the slum.

The film opens in the 1960s near Cidade de Deus. People live in the *favelas* because they are so poor they have no other place to go. Three teenagers decide to rob a truck that sells gasoline. These three are small-time criminals who commit mostly robberies and then share their gains with the people in the *favela*. Some of the younger children in the slum want to get involved in the crimes as well. Here, two of the main characters of the film are introduced, Zé Pequeno, (or Lil Zé), and his friend Bené. Lil Zé has no conscience or scruples and decides to get into the action with the older boys. The three older teenagers decide later to carry out a robbery on at a local hotel while Lil Zé is left to stand guard. When the teenagers leave the hotel with some money, Lil Zé enters the hotel and kills as many people as he can. Finally, the other principle character in the film, Rocket, is introduced. He is the younger brother of one of the three

FIGURE 11.1 Lil Zé in *Cidade de Deus* (2002, Miramax).

older teenagers, and he is told by Lil Zé that he is smart and needs to study and not get involved in the drugs and violence in the *favela*. Here the film sets up the dichotomy of the lives of Rocket and Lil Zé, both of whom live in the *favela* and both of whom will take very different courses in life. Both are trying to survive in their surroundings. Only one will make it out alive.

There is no police force to speak of in the slums. Law enforcement is carried out by ordinary men with guns. They are corrupt—drug dealers, burglars, and murderers—and in order to stay on their good side, the people have to pay them "protection" money. Eventually the three teenagers are discovered and their role at a hotel massacre is broadcast, even though they didn't take place in the killings. One of the boys turns to the Church for help. Another is shot while trying to escape. The third boy attempts to rob Lil Zé, but gets killed by Lil Zé instead. Now that the three teenagers are gone, it is time for Lil Zé and the younger boys to become the crime leaders in the *favela*.

In the 1970s, Cidade de Deus has grown considerably. It has become an even more dangerous place where drugs, prostitution, and violence abound. Lil Zé is older now and decides to make money dealing drugs. In order to make more money, he kills or has killed most of the other dealers in the favela and takes their business for himself, eliminating his competition. Now he and his boyhood friend Bené run the City of God like their own little kingdom. Zé also begins to train young boys in the business; they act as couriers and messengers for Zé and learn the ins and outs of the drug trade. At one juncture, Zé orders one of the "Runts" as they are called to kill a little kid in order to be initiated into the group. They boy complies.

Eventually, Bené, Zé's friend, decides to leave the business and get clean. He wants to get out of the crime and drug dealing and move on with his life. But Zé is not pleased by this decision and as Bené is the only person who can exercise even a little control over Zé's sociopathic behavior, his decision to leave sets the stage for much violence and brutality in the *favela*. At Bené's going-away party, he gives a camera to Rocket. This has been Rocket's dream for a long time and he is very pleased. But in the midst of the celebration, tragedy strikes, as Bené is shot to death by a rival drug dealer.

From this point on, Zé is out of control and the violence in the *favela* and portrayed on the screen increases dramatically. At the same time, Rocket tries desperately to escape from the City of God and become a newspaper photographer. As the violence escalates and Zé moves closer and closer to the edge of insanity, Rocket miraculously gets a job taking photographs for a local newspaper. His employers pressure him to return to the *favela* to take photographs of the people, lifestyle, and gangs. But Rocket is afraid to return now that he has made his way out. Eventually, Rocket does return and finds himself directly in the middle of a gang war between Zé's followers and a rival gang. Rocket takes some photos that become famous because no one has ever photographed the gangs in the City of God, or Zé himself.

The film closes with Zé on the run. He is trying to escape the vendetta of the other drug lords in the *favela* that have overpowered his own gang. As Zé tries to escape, he runs into the Runts, the young boys he was training to move into his gang when they got older. When the Runts realize that Zé is in trouble, they simply shoot him multiple times and then easily walk away. Rocket takes some final photographs and then leaves the City of God for good.

When *Cidade de Deus* came out in 2002, viewers were amazed by the graphic violence present in the *favelas* in Brazil, and the lifestyle of the people who lived there. The film increased people's awareness of the way of life of the poorest of the poor in Latin America and the struggles they deal with on a daily basis. While the film was based loosely on actual events and people, some of the production was dramatized, but these elements emphasized the life and struggles of the people in these poverty-stricken parts of Brazil. The film was nominated for many awards including four Academy Awards and a Golden Globe. For years to come, *Cidade de Deus* will remain a powerful example of modern Latin American history on film.

Men With Guns (1997)

Men With Guns (1997) is a film about a medical doctor in an unnamed Latin American country. The movie was filmed in Mexico, and in addition to Spanish, several Native American dialects are spoken in the film including Kuna, Nahuatl, and Tzotzil, all either Mayan or Central Mexican languages. Nevertheless, the location of the drama is never revealed. Written and directed by John Sayles,

Men With Guns contemplates the power of legacy and the effects that a single individual can have on the lives of countless others.

Dr. Humberto Fuentes is a medical doctor, living comfortably in a large city in a Latin American country. His wife has recently died and he believes that he is at the end of his career. He begins to contemplate his contributions to humanity and the people of his country. He decides that his greatest legacy is the ongoing work of seven medical students he trained years earlier. In addition to their medical training, he taught these seven that ignorance is like a disease and can infect anyone. This of course foreshadows his own ignorance regarding the conditions of the poor and indigenous in his own country. His former students have gone into the countryside and the mountains to work among the poor and destitute. Dr. Fuentes decides that he will travel into the interior of the country and seek out his former students so that he can behold with satisfaction the fruits of their—and by association his—labors.

As he makes his way inland, he first encounters a former student who went into the mountains to be a medical doctor for the poor. Now, however, this student has become a smuggler running a black market pharmacy. Dr. Fuentes' student is bitter and tells his former professor that he, Fuentes, is ignorant of what is really going on in the country, and that his ideological visions are naïve at best. Troubled, Fuentes continues on his journey to find the others. At this juncture, he meets an American couple who are touring the interior of the country, complete with backpacks and guidebooks. As he talks to them, it becomes strikingly clear that they know more about the atrocities and political injustices in his country than he does.

He leaves them and makes his way to a village where no one will speak with him, likely because they speak an Indian dialect instead of Spanish. Eventually, he finds someone willing to talk to him in exchange for some medical help. He learns that the people of the village did know one of his students, but that student was murdered by "men with guns" sometime ago. Fuentes is beginning to understand the difference between the poor who are trying to feed themselves, the guerrilla factions in the jungle who fight for "freedom," and the government troops who enforce the political power of the regime.

Fuentes leaves the village disturbed. He treks to another indigenous village where once again no one will speak with him except a young boy. The boy explains to Fuentes that indeed there was a young doctor in the village a while ago, but the army came and took him away, apparently because he was aiding the rebels who fight against the government. The boy shows Dr. Fuentes a nearby location where dozens of people were massacred by the army for being subversives. Fuentes is stunned and remarks that he didn't know about any of this. He asks the boy how the people of the village survive, and is told that they grow coffee and sell it for food, illuminating their neocolonial economic relationship with their own government.

In due course, Fuentes encounters some soldiers. He is told by the boy that the soldiers will probably kill him because he is a stranger. When he observes that most of the soldiers are in fact Native American Indians, he asks why there are no white soldiers. He is told that when an Indian puts on a uniform, he becomes white. Within moments, one of the soldiers robs Fuentes, taking his money and the tires from his vehicle. Stranded and wondering what to do, Fuentes waits and eventually the same soldier returns wounded. He gives the tires back, and Fuentes treats him the best that he can with his limited resources. Then Fuentes, the soldier, and the indigenous boy all travel together to another town. In this location, Fuentes finds out that yet another of his students had been in this location but had recently been murdered by the guerrillas because he treated the soldiers when they came through the village. Here, Fuentes realizes that the conflict and chaos in his country make little sense. If a doctor helps the guerrillas, or even the indigenous, he is killed by the army. If he helps the army, he is killed by the guerrillas.

Dr. Fuentes and his retinue continue on and eventually pick up a hitchhiker who turns out to be a former priest who has lost his faith. He joins this strange group of companions and tells of his journey to faithlessness. His story represents the journey Fuentes himself is taking from obliviousness, to incredulity, to outrage. The priest tells of how in the not too distant past, he lived in a village with the Indian population. The army came and accused the village of aiding the guerrillas. When the villagers protest that this was untrue, the soldiers tell the villagers to kill three people including the priest. But the villagers are unable to comply because the priest runs away. The soldiers return and kill almost all of the people in the village. This is the reason that the priest has lost his faith. He is wracked with guilt over the slayings, and is also angry with God for allowing such a thing to happen.

Eventually, Fuentes and his strange companions, now joined by a woman who survived a rape but has now become mute as a result of the abuse of her torturers, are stopped at an army checkpoint. The priest is immediately taken into custody and presumably shot (reflecting the same attitudes presented in the film *Romero*, where priests who help the indigenous and poor are viewed as subversives and enemies of the state). Despairing, Dr. Fuentes decides to search for the last of his students, a female doctor who is purported to live high up in the mountains in a hidden village. The group hikes through the jungle, encounter the American tourists once again, and then arrive at a small village. When Fuentes learns that this is not the village where the female doctor lives, he sits down next to a tree and declares that his legacy is nothing. None of his students are alive except for the pharmacy smuggler and supposedly the female doctor who cannot be found. As his traveling companions debate what to do next, Fuentes mysteriously dies, feeling like a failure.

The storyline of *Men With Guns* could have taken place in many different parts of Latin America, from Argentina to Bolivia and Peru in South America, to Guatemala and Honduras in Central America. Part of the value of the film is its ability to apply this situation to many different locations throughout Latin

America where corrupt governments oppress their populations, and where armed resistance in the countryside attempts to fight that oppression. And as always, stuck in the middle are the poor, the indigenous, and the illiterate minorities who suffer the most from the violence, poverty, and corruption that encompass their lives. Jack Mathews reviewed *Men With Guns* for the *Los Angeles Times* in 1998. And while he appraises the film positively, he also makes the connections that the director Sayles is trying to present to the viewer.

> Sayles opens the film with a scene of a native woman telling her young daughter about a city doctor who can heal by touch. He's a sick man, fighting for his breath in the high mountain air . . . and as Fuentes' small party trudges through the jungles, looking for a rumored paradise away from politics and war, the connection becomes clear. But it's a weak connection, too facile for the kind of epiphany Sayles has in mind. *Men With Guns* is strong enough on its own. It doesn't need a higher power.

Notes

1 Mark P. Sullivan and June S. Beittel, *Latin America: Terrorism Issues*, Congressional Research and Service Report for Congress, April 5, 2013, 3.
2 Sullivan, 24–25.
3 Janice Perlman, *Favela*, Oxford University Press, 2010, 27.

Further Reading

Dueñas, Gabriela Polit and María Helena Rueda (eds), *Meanings of Violence in Contemporary Latin America*. London: Palgrave Macmillan, 2011.

Esparza, Marcia, et al. *State Violence and Genocide in Latin America: The Cold War Years*. New York and London: Routledge, 2011.

Fowler, Will. *Political Violence and the Construction of National Identity in Latin America*. London: Palgrave Macmillan, 2006.

Grandin, Greg and Gilbert M. Joseph (eds). *A Century of Revolution: Insurgent and Counterinsurgent Violence During Latin America's Long Cold War*. Durham, NC: Duke University Press, 2010.

Perlman, Janice. *Favela*. Oxford: Oxford University Press, 2010.

Rosenberg, Tina *Children of Cain: Violence and the Violent in Latin America*, London: Penguin Books, 1992.

Sullivan, Mark P. and June S. Beittel. *Latin America: Terrorism Issues*. Congressional Research and Service Report for Congress, April 5 2013.

Wickham-Crowley, Timothy P. *Guerrillas and Revolution in Latin America*. Princeton, NJ: Princeton University Press, 1993.

12

LATINO CULTURE IN THE UNITED STATES

I received a letter just before I left office from a man. He wrote that you can go to live in France, but you can't become a Frenchman. You can go to live in Germany or Italy, but you can't become a German, an Italian. He went through Turkey, Greece, Japan, and other countries. But he said anyone from any corner of the world, can come to live in the United States and become an American.

Ronald Reagan

Introduction

For centuries, Latin America has been viewed by the United States as an exotic American backyard where banana republics existed and backward nations survived, where Americans traveled for vacation, and where US businesses took control of entire governments. But during the last half of the twentieth century, Latin Americans from many different countries entered the United States in ever increasing numbers, and began to challenge these old notions and stereotypes of Latin American countries. They fill jobs, go to school, serve in the military, and are increasingly involved in economics and politics. It should be no surprise that one of the largest Spanish-speaking populations in the world resides inside the United States, with a population of nearly 50 million people (second only to Mexico with a population of nearly 120 million people).

The United States shares a border with Mexico that is roughly 2000 miles long. This border is one of the most unique locations on the planet; where a highly developed nation and a struggling, developing nation meet and interact. But the US–Mexican border is not just a place where two different cultures meet—they overlap there. Some have used tongue-in-cheek phrases such as "Mex-America" or "Amexica." But the truth is that this is the location of economic, social, and cultural interactions where two cultures have coexisted for hundreds of years.

Latinos in the United States

During World War II, so many young American men were called into military service that the agricultural sector in the US began to suffer. In 1942, the US government agreed with Mexico to allow a few thousand Mexican agricultural laborers to enter the US to offset the continuing and growing labor shortages. These laborers were called *Braceros* (laborers). By the end of World War II, around 50000 *Braceros* were working in agricultural production all across the United States. Frequently, the *Braceros* entered the US alone without their families, but as time went on, communities of *Braceros* and their family members began to grow in various US states.

Following the war, significant numbers of *Bracero* workers were permitted to remain in the US throughout the 1950s and 1960s. Numbers eventually grew to more than 400000 laborers in the United States by the end of the 1950s. The total number of *Braceros* who entered the US between 1942 and 1964 is estimated at more than four million. But not everyone was pleased with the increasing numbers of Mexican laborers and their families who entered and resided in the US and in 1954 Operation Wetback was responsible for deporting more than one million Mexicans out of the US and back into Mexico. But hundreds of thousands of Mexican workers and their families continued to remain in the US instead of returning to Mexico during the colder winter months. Because of the *Bracero* Program, Mexican laborers were able to bring in enough money to survive on in the US, with enough left over to send to family members who lived in Mexico.

When the *Bracero* Program ended in the mid-1960s, many Mexican families found ways to remain in the US and not be sent back to Mexico. In fact, thousands of Mexican Americans today can trace their US roots to the Bracero Program in the middle of the twentieth century.

In the early 1990s, construction of a barrier began in some places along the US–Mexican border. In California the "fence," as it is called, separated Tijuana from San Diego. The wall is constructed of corrugated steel and is roughly ten feet high. In other locations along the border, the wall is made of concrete, chain-link, or barbed wire. And in some locations there is no fence or barrier of any kind. An army of Border Patrol agents use helicopters, trucks, computers, motion-detecting sensors, and video cameras to find and catch those who try to enter the United States illegally. But these measures do not stop individuals and families from many Latin American countries from coming into the US in the thousands every year.

According to the 2010 US Census, of the nearly 50 million people in the United States that come from a Latino background, 63 percent are of Mexican origin. Another 9 percent are of Puerto Rican background, 3.5 percent are Cuban, just over 3 percent are Salvadoran, and the remainder comes from various Central and South American countries. By the year 2050, according to the US Census Bureau, the Latino population of the United States is estimated to be just under 130 million people, and will constitute around 30 percent of the population of the United States. Sixteen US states count a Latino population of more than half a million residents, and in New Mexico the percentage in the state is around 46 percent, the highest of any state, followed closely by California and Texas with just under 40 percent each. Several cities in the US count Latino populations of well over a million residents: Los Angeles contains the highest number with around six million, or 45 percent of the population of the city; New York City has more than four million, or 25 percent; and Houston has around two million or just under 40 percent.[1]

Over the past five and a half decades since the 1960s, the predominant Mexican and Puerto Rican populations in the US have been augmented by millions of people from all over Latin America. And, "as these populations have expanded and become more geographically dispersed, Latinos of all national origins, heritages, and class backgrounds now reside and intermingle in a broad range of different urban and rural settings in communities across the United States."[2]

Why? Why are so many Latin Americans trying to come into the United States? In 1965, the Immigration and Nationality Act passed by the US Congress eliminated many of the restrictive quotas on how many Latin Americans and other foreign-born immigrants could enter the US, which had been in place since the beginning of the twentieth century. The Immigration and Nationality Act made it much easier for foreign-born peoples to immigrate to the United States. Previously, populations from other countries had been severely restricted in their ability to settle in the US, and this Act made it possible for many more immigrant populations to enter the US than ever before. In answer to the question posed above, much of the immigration is driven by laborers in search of better wages, higher standards of living, and the opportunity to live a better life. But people in the United States often cannot see the poverty that brings Latin Americans to the US. This begs the question, what do Americans see? More often than not, Americans only see gangs, unmarried mothers, drugs, illegal crossers, and populations that do not easily assimilate into mainstream American culture.

As mentioned above, the majority of the foreign-born Latin American population in the US has come from Mexico. But increasing numbers of immigrants from Central and South America continue to augment these numbers. From Central America, more individuals from El Salvador and Guatemala have entered the US than from the other Central American nations. And from South America, Colombia and Peru contribute the largest numbers of US immigrants. In addition, the numbers of Latino immigrants from the Caribbean have also increased in the US, with most people coming from the Dominican Republic and Cuba. These émigrés have joined the large and growing Latino and Hispanic populations in the US who come from Latin American immigrant stock, but are native-born US citizens. Scholars have noted that these people play, and will continue to play, an important role in US demographics, because even if immigration levels decline, rates of natural increase will continue to contribute to the growth and development of these populations.

Latino culture in the United States is becoming more flexible and accommodating than in previous generations, and this stems from its collective cultural contact with mainstream American culture. Cultural stereotypes of the past, including the idea that Latinos were more passive, more fatalistic, and more family-oriented have now given way to more cosmopolitan views of Latinos in the US, and important population shifts have shaped Latino culture into more regional and class-oriented formations than one single overarching Latino society within the borders of the US.

In fact, recently, the history of Latinos in the US has begun to resemble in some ways the history of African Americans during the Civil Rights Movement. As Latinos fight for rights in the US, they combat many of the same battles that were fought by generations of different ethnic and racial groups throughout United States history including émigrés from European countries such as Germany, Ireland, Poland, and Russia, and immigrants from Asian countries such as Korea, Vietnam, China, and Japan. But the historical relationships that have shaped relations between the United States and Latin America have also affected the way Latinos express themselves in the US. Unlike immigrants from Western Europe during previous centuries, Latin Americans have not assimilated into American culture and society to the same degree and become part of the great "melting pot" that is America. This displacement is experienced both physically and geographically, but also psychologically and culturally as well.[3] This is significant because it in effect causes the displacement of Latinos from their own cultural heritage while at the same time depriving them of cultural expression in the US, leaving them somewhere in the middle. As Edward James Olmos says in the film *Selena* (1997):

> We are Mexican-Americans . . . Being Mexican-American is tough. Anglos jump all over you if you don't speak English perfectly. Mexicans jump all over you if you don't speak Spanish perfectly. We gotta be twice as perfect as anybody else . . . Japanese-Americans, Italian-Americans, German Americans, their homeland is on the other side of the ocean. Ours is right next door. Right over there. And we gotta prove to the Mexicans how Mexican we are. And we gotta prove to the Americans how American we are. We gotta be more Mexican than the Mexicans and more American than the Americans both at the same time. It's exhausting! Damn! Nobody knows how tough it is to be a Mexican-American!

Filmography

Selecting films for this chapter was challenging. There is no end to the number of films made over the past several decades that portray Latino culture in the United States. Just a few of the films that could have been included in this chapter include: *The Milagro Beanfield War* (1988), *Tortilla Soup* (2001), *Tortilla Heaven* (2007), *And the Earth Did Not Swallow Him* (1994), *Mano a Mano* (2005), and *La Bamba* (1987). In determining which titles to include here, several factors had to be taken into account such as the conflict between American and Latino cultures and values, the ways Latinos deal with bigotry and racism in the US, and the stereotypical ways many Americans view and interact with individuals from Latino communities.

With these criteria in mind, three films are included in the filmography for this chapter: *Selena* (1997), *Real Women Have Curves* (2002), and *My Family* (1995). All three capture the frustrations and successes inherent in Latino culture inside the United States. *Selena* is a biopic based on the life of Tejano singer Selena Quintanilla-Pérez in Texas. It recounts her rise to fame, struggles to be accepted in both Mexican and American society, and her untimely death in 1995. *Real Women Have Curves*, while fictional, discusses the situation of Latina women in some parts of the US, and the struggles they endure that are not even on the radar of American teens and women. Finally, *My Family* presents a generational view of life as a Latino family in Los Angeles. This film progresses from the first generation that arrived in the US and struggled to make ends meet, all the while fearing deportation, to the next generation as their children enter adulthood, and finally to the final generation when the children are adults, making their own decisions, and trying to help and understand their own children. This film is unique in that it portrays not only the chronology of a fictional Latino family living in southern California, but it also shines light on the influences that living in the United States has on a Latino family through time and from one generation to another.

All three films represent a different element and aspect of the life of Latinos in the US, and each highlights not only the negatives and struggles, but also the victories and successes of individuals trying to live in a dissimilar culture while remaining true to their own ethnic identities.

Selena *(1997)*

Gregory Nava's 1997 film *Selena* depicts the life and tragic death of Selena Quintanilla-Pérez, a Tejano music sensation in Texas and Mexico in the mid-1990s. Filmed just two years after her murder, *Selena* takes the viewer through Selena's life from the time she was a little girl, through her rise to stardom, and to her appalling death in 1995.

The film opens on Selena (Jennifer Lopez) and her band playing to a sold-out crowd at the Houston Astrodome in 1995. This scene sets the stage for the rest of the film, which flashes back to 1961 when her father, Abraham Quintanilla (Edward James Olmos) and two other fellows formed a singing trio focused on traditional jazz-pop music, despite the fact that they were all of Mexican origin. Because of their Mexican heritage, the band was panned and remained unsuccessful. This flashback shows the racial and ethnic persecution minorities in Texas and the United States faced at this time.

The film then jumps to 1981 when Selena's father starts having her sing and, realizing her talent, forms a new band consisting of Selena and her brother and sister. Finding venues where they can perform is somewhat challenging, so Selena's father decides to open a Mexican restaurant where the kids can sing on stage while people eat. Soon the restaurant goes bankrupt, however, and the family is forced to move. But Selena's father Abraham continues to encourage his children to pursue musical careers. Selena begins to learn Spanish so that she can sing to the Spanish-speaking population of Texas as well, and her father tells her that she needs to come to terms with her identity as an American who is also a Mexican.

By 1989, the group of siblings is having more success singing Tejano music, a genre that mixes popular American and Mexican elements with some jazz and folk influences as well. Around this time, the band hires a guitar player named Chris Pérez to augment the sound of the band, and he begins to have a relationship with Selena. Soon, Selena's father decides that the band should cross the border and play in Mexico. He warns Selena that the Mexican culture will be foreign to her, and she will be expected to speak good Spanish and to prove how "Mexican" she is. While in Monterrey, Mexico, the band is a huge success and this adds to Selena's popularity on both sides of the border.

FIGURE 12.1 Jennifer Lopez and James Edward Olmos in *Selena* (1997, Warner Bros).

Despite the growing success of the band, tensions within the group flare as Selena's father and guitarist Chris Pérez clash. At the height of the tension, Chris is fired from the band, but then he and Selena secretly elope and get married. The family eventually comes to terms with the marriage and returns to focusing on the band and its future. Selena plans to release an English-language crossover album that will permit her to enter mainstream American music culture. She also begins a boutique and clothing line, and plays some minor roles on television programs. Then, at the zenith of her success, she is nominated for and wins a Grammy Award for Best Mexican-American Album in 1994.

However, problems emerge with the finances of her brand, including the clothing line and her earnings from her music. Soon, Selena and her father learn that her fan-club manager, Yolanda Saldívar, has been embezzling funds, writing false checks, and mismanaging other aspects of the band and Selena's other endeavors. On March 31, 1995, Selena confronted Saldívar at a Corpus Christi hotel, demanding paperwork and the return of the money. During the confrontation, Saldívar produced a handgun and shot Selena. Selena was rushed to a local hospital where she was pronounced dead.

The legacy of Selena, both as a singer and an entrepreneur, is portrayed well in the film, showing the difficulties that minorities, particularly Mexican Americans, face living in the United States. Aside from her music and other activities, Selena became a model for other Latinos in the US who struggled for inclusion in American culture and society. Her untimely death elevated her to even higher status as a symbol of that assimilation between cultures, and she remains an icon for both American and Mexican societal traditions.

Real Women Have Curves *(2002)*

Real Women Have Curves (2002) is the fictional story of a Mexican American family living in Los Angeles, California. The film follows Ana (America Ferrera) who has just completed high school. But instead of going to college, her traditional Latina mother wants her to stay home and work to support the family. Ana is bitter about the expectations her family has of her, but begins working at a sewing factory where high-end dresses are produced.

In the factory, Ana works with her mother and sister, and some other Latina women who have known each other for many years. Ana resents having to spend time in the factory, and her mother shames her into continuing to work there by stating that in their family everyone works, and it is her duty to work for the family instead of selfishly going off to college. In a pique of rebellion, Ana burns an expensive dress with an iron, much to the anger and distress of her mother. The film portrays Ana's mother as a stereotypical Latina woman complete with over-exaggeration and drama, all because of an unspoken desire not to lose her last child to adulthood. Here, the film develops the theme of familial solidarity in Latino communities, and the perceived lack of such values in American households. Ana's mother feels that if Ana goes away to college, she will lose some of her Latino heritage.

Eventually, some of the women at the dress factory announce that they are leaving and returning to Mexico, which will leave the factory short-handed and unable to meet their quota with the supplier. Now, they will not be able to pay their rent on the property and will most likely be evicted. While these external pressures grow, the struggle between Ana and her mother intensifies. In a dramatic effort to get more attention from her daughter, Ana's mother starts to believe that she, the mother, is pregnant. But Ana is having none of it and begins to spend time with a boy from her school days.

During the summer, Ana learns that she has been accepted into Columbia University on a full scholarship. She is very excited, but her family is not, and they fear that Ana leaving would be a step toward breaking up the family. In frustration, Ana spends more time with her boyfriend, losing her virginity along the way. When her mother finds out, the rift between the two grows even wider.

The film moves to conclusion as Ana and the few remaining employees at the dress factory finish a critical dress order, wearing only their underwear because it is so hot in the factory. Ana's mother thinks they have all gone crazy. Once the pressure of the dress order and the rent is dealt with, Ana returns to her ambition to attend Columbia University. Finally, her decision made, she prepares to leave home. Her mother refuses to say goodbye to her, feigning illness. The rest of the family wishes her well, and the film closes with Ana walking in New York City and beginning a new chapter of her life.

Elvis Mitchell reviewed *Real Women Have Curves* for the *New York Times* in 2002. He observed that the film presents the "generational conflict . . . between the Blossoming Ana . . . and her mother, who is determined that Ana follow convention and go to work with her in a Los Angeles sweatshop." Mitchell discerns that the film sets up conflict between Ana and her mother, two strong-willed women, while at the same time not coloring the mother "unequivocally as a heartless villain."

My Family (1995)

Like *Selena*, *My Family* was directed by Gregory Nava and was released in 1995. The film is a big-picture look at a Latino family in Los Angeles over a three-generation time period. Many stereotypes about Mexican Americans are visible in the movie, but the struggles for identity and against assimilation are at the forefront throughout the film.

The story begins in Mexico a couple of decades after the ousting of dictator Porfirio Díaz in 1911. A man named José decides that he will walk to Los Angeles in California in order to make more money to support the family that will remain behind in Mexico. After traveling for a year, he arrives in Los Angeles in the early 1930s and begins making a new life for himself. He takes a job doing manual labor and landscaping, along with other Mexican American immigrants. While working, he meets a young Mexican American woman and the two are soon married and expecting a child. José begins to cultivate corn and beans on their small property near their house in order to provide more food for the growing family.

One day, José's wife María doesn't come home from the market. While making purchases, she was rounded up by the military along with other illegal immigrants, and deported to Mexico, even though she was a US citizen. Now in Mexico, and unable to cross back into the US, María travels to Central Mexico to live with her extended family. She remains with her family in Mexico until her child is born, and then she begins the long walk north to attempt to reenter the US. When she arrives in Los Angeles, she introduces her new son Chucho to his father José.

By 1958, the children are growing up and becoming adults. The family is preparing a wedding for one of the daughters, and father José has spent way too much money on the arrangements. In the midst of the celebrations, a Latino gang comes to the house looking to make trouble with Chucho, who now belongs to a rival gang. Not long after this altercation, José realizes that his son Chucho is selling drugs for cash. They clash over dignity and the value of honor, but eventually realize that they are from two very different worlds. José represents much of traditional Mexican values, family solidarity, and honor, while Chucho has grown up in Los Angeles and does not hold these same values, having not grown up in Mexico. José worked hard his whole life, but Chucho wants an easy ride. José eventually kicks Chucho out of the house.

Later, Chucho gets into a knife fight with the leader of the rival gang and ends up killing him. Chucho runs from the police as his family becomes frantic. Chucho's youngest brother Jimmy finds him and tries to help him, but the police soon find them and shoot Chucho, killing him right in front of Jimmy. This middle section of the film ends with the family in turmoil and grief at the loss of Chucho, and the conflict rising in young Jimmy after seeing the death of his older brother.

In 1978, Jimmy has grown up and is in jail for armed robbery. He has become an angry loner. He refuses to spend time with his family after being released from his incarceration. Soon, his older sister Toni, who is a nun, announces to the family that she has renounced her vows and married a former priest, who is an American, and who has also renounced his vows. This plot twist brings an element of ethnic diversity into the family structure, but everyone seems to take the dynamics of the marriage in stride. Toni and her new husband begin working in an agency that helps immigrants and illegal aliens in the United States who face deportation and other problems. Toni begins working with a woman from El Salvador named Isabel who will soon be deported. Toni approaches her younger brother Jimmy and asks him to marry Isabel to keep her from being deported. After a loud argument, Jimmy relents and agrees to marry the girl, but he will have nothing else to do with her. That evening, María, the aging mother, tells her family that her children, the younger generation, have lost their traditional Mexican family values and respect for the sacred things in life such as marriage. Eventually, Jimmy begins to fall in love with Isabel despite his earlier inclinations, and they begin a life together.

Jimmy starts to turn his life around; he gets a job and begins to feel more responsible, especially because Isabel is pregnant. But tragedy strikes when Isabel hemorrhages during labor and dies, leaving behind a baby boy named Carlos. Jimmy loses control of himself and his life, and soon gets incarcerated for armed robbery. While in jail, an American guard who knew Jimmy the last time he was in prison remarks that he knew Jimmy would return because "your kind always comes back," indicating Jimmy's Latino heritage. While Jimmy is in prison, his son Carlos is raised by José and María.

After several years, Jimmy returns home to his mother and father, and his son Carlos who he has never known. Jimmy tells his father he is going away to get a fresh start, but José reminds him that he is a father now and has responsibilities at home. So, despite the fact that young Carlos wants absolutely nothing to do with him, Jimmy decides to stay and patiently wait for Carlos to accept him as his father.

At this point, another of José and María's sons, Memo, brings his American fiancée home to meet the family. At no other point in the film are the stark differences between American and Latino cultures in the US portrayed as well. Memo has gone to school and become an attorney. His fiancée's parents are interested in meeting Memo's family, but they quickly become uncomfortable at their apparent poverty. Memo becomes increasingly ashamed of his heritage, and tries to actively diminish his ties to his family in front of his soon-to-be in-laws. After several awkward exchanges, little Carlos runs into the room naked and the in-laws abruptly leave. Memo decides to leave his past life and culture behind and he chooses to live in a more Americanized world.

The film concludes with Jimmy and little Carlos becoming reconciled to each other. And as the film draws to a close, José and María reminisce about what a good life they have had. Despite the troubles, problems, heartaches, and dilemmas, they have also had moments of happiness and joy with their children and now grandchildren. Somehow, they managed to live their entire adult lives in the US without compromising their traditional Mexican values. And even though their children and grandchildren have grown up with American influences all around them, they have, in many ways, retained at their core their Mexican heritage and the conventional values that made it possible for them to live as Mexican Americans in the United States.

In 1995, Roger Ebert summed up the film nicely when he wrote, "it is an epic told through the eyes of one family, the Sanchez family, whose father walked north to Los Angeles from Mexico . . . and whose children include a writer, a nun, an ex-convict, a lawyer, a restaurant owner, and a boy shot dead in his prime." Ebert concludes his review with praise for the film, stating, "few movies like this get made because few filmmakers have the ambition to open their arms wide and embrace so much life . . . Rarely have I felt at the movies such a sense of time and history, of stories and lessons passing down the generations, of a family living in its memories."

Notes

1 Population statistics retrieved from the US Census Bureau, and the Pew Research Center.
2 David G. Gutiérrez, ed., *The Columbia History of Latinos in the United States Since 1960*, Columbia University Press, 2004, 2.
3 Gutiérrez, 355.

Further Reading

Chaves, Leo R. *The Latino Threat: Constructing Immigrants, Citizens, and the Nation.* Chicago, IL: Stanford University Press, 2008.

Dávila, Arlene. *Latino Spin: Public Image and the Whitewashing of Race.* New York: New York University Press, 2008.

Gonzalez, Juan. *Harvest of Empire: A History of Latinos in America.* London: Penguin Books, 2011.

Gutiérrez, David G. *The Columbia History of Latinos in the United States since 1960.* New York: Columbia University Press, 2004.

Roll, Samuel. *The Invisible Border: Latinos in America.* London: Nicholas Brealey Publishing, 2008.

Shorris, Earl. *Latinos: A Biography of the People.* New York: W.W. Norton, 2001.

Urrea, Luis Alberto. *The Devil's Highway.* New York: Back Bay Books, 2005.

INDEX